A Grim Almanac of
South Yorkshire

Matthew Hopkins, Witch Finder Generall, pictured on a woodcut that accompanied his book,
The Discovery of Witches. (Mansell Collection)

A Grim Almanac of
South Yorkshire

Kevin Turton

The
History
Press

The Grim Almanacs
are from an original idea by Neil R. Storey

First published 2004
This edition published 2010

The History Press
The Mill, Brimscombe Port
Stroud, Gloucestershire, GL5 2QG
www.thehistorypress.co.uk

British Library Cataloguing in Publication Data.
A catalogue record for this book is available from the British Library.

ISBN 978 0 7524 5678 2

Typesetting and origination by The History Press
Printed in Great Britain

Endpapers. Front: The funeral of the
Kimberworth murders victims, 20
November 1912.
(Rotherham Archives and Local Studies)
Back: A woodcut of the Rotherham boat
disaster.
(Rotherham Archives and Local Studies)

CONTENTS

THE LAST DYING SPEECH AND CONFESSION

Of SPENCE BROUGHTON, JOHN LUCAS, THOMAS STEARMAN, JOSEPH BREARLY & THOMAS CRAWSHAW.

Who were executed To Day at TYBURN near YORK.

SPENCE BROUGHTON aged 46 was born near Marton in Lincolnshire, of respectable parents who gave him a fair education, and brought him up in a very indulgent manner; at the age of 22, his father placed him in a farm, and stocked it with every thing necessary, he married the only daughter of a respectable farmer in the neighbourhood, with whom he received a considerable fortune, which he spent in riot and debauchery, neglecting his business, which caused a disagreement to happen between him and his wife, he left her and went to London, where he got acquainted with Shaw, Close, and Oxley, to whom, (whatever his crimes before,) he may certainly attribute his fatal end.

He was indicted for stopping the post boy, carrying the mail from Sheffield to Rotherham, and feloniously taking away the said mail, containing letters, in one of which was inclosed a French bill of exchange, drawn by a merchant in France, on the house of Minnet & Fector in London, payable to Mr Joseph Walker of Rotherham, for 123l. or thereabouts. Thomas Shaw, an accomplice, (admitted an evidence) proved that some days after the above robbery, Broughton sent for him, and told him that he and Oxley had robbed the said mail; that he being taken lame at Mansfield, was unable to proceed further at that time, that Oxley had come forward with the bill, to London, and desired to know if Shaw had seen Oxley, and whether he knew how the bill was disposed of. Shaw then informed him that by the help of a French dictionary they had made out on whom the bill was drawn, that Oxley had procured a person for five guineas to forge the indorsement of Mr. Walker and then sent by a porter at the Temple gate for payment. Broughton then said Oxley was a villain, that he had only left 10l. with his woman, as his share; on asking where Oxley was, and being answered gone to Leicester cocking, he swore he would go after him, and if he refused to give him his due share he would take it from him. Broughton after this got 40l. as his share, from Oxley declaring that he had given the man who forged the indorsement twenty guineas, and other sum which brought his share to that sum

evidence, as his evidence was given very collected and clear.----The Judge then summed up the evidence, and the jury after a very short consultation found the prisoner *Guilty*. The Judge then pronounced sentence on him that he should be hanged and afterwards hung in chains, near the place where the robbery was committed. the prisoner during the awful sentence distinguished himself by as firm and manly demeanour, and bowed to the court with a degree of fortitude and resignation which evinced his sincere intention of dedicating the short remains of his life towards imploring forgiveness of that *all merciful Judge to whom alone he is now accountable.*

Since his condemnation he has behaved himself with a manly fortitude, and has taken great pains with his fellow sufferers, in order to bring them to repentance, he made no confession, but died in peace with all men, forgiving those who had swore away his life to save themselves. His only support during his confinement was sent him by *Mrs Hill* with whom he cohabited, in *London*. When he was apprehended, the Bow-street officers took a considerable sum from him, which they have appropriated to their own use.

John Lucas, and Thomas Stearman, were indicted for breaking open the shop of Messrs. Mundels of Malton, and stealing thereout goods to the amount of 700l. the principal evidence was one. Walker an accomplice. They acknowledged the justice of their sentence, but refused to confess the particular crimes they had committed, which were too enormous, and might bring others into the same predicament, to the utter ruin of themselves and families. *Lucas* was by trade a mason; aged about 40, has left a wife and family to deplore his untimely fate. *Stearman* was about the same age, by trade a Staymaker, but neglecting his business, took to vicious courses which brought him to an untimely end.

The dying speech of Spence Broughton, John Lucas, Thomas Stearman, Joseph Brearly and Thomas Crawshaw, 15 April 1792 (see 7 February). *(Sheffield Libraries, Archives and Local Studies)*

ACKNOWLEDGEMENTS

I am deeply indebted to the following, without whom this book would not have been completed nor would it have told so grim a tale. The staff of the Sheffield section of the Local Studies Library without whom I would have floundered in the dark; the superb help of Doncaster Archives where nothing was ever too difficult to find; Anthony Munford who died recently and whose help, knowledge and expertise, not only in the writing of this book but also in past enterprises, have been unstinting; the staff of Rotherham Archives and Local Studies who were tireless in their help and for whom nothing was ever too much trouble; Doncaster Local Studies Library for helping to guide me through the town's rich and varied past; and the authors of the following magazines whose extensive knowledge of dark and murky deeds have proved a rich source of both material and inspiration: the *Ivanhoe Review*, the *Gentleman's Review*, the *Gentleman's Magazine*, *Burland's Annals of Barnsley*, *Sheffield Local Register*, *Thorne Monthly Illustrated*, *Historical Notices of Doncaster* and of course those hundreds of anonymous newspaper reporters who worked on the *Rotherham Advertiser*, the *Sheffield Mercury*, the *Sheffield and Rotherham Independent*, the *Yorkshire and Derbyshire Independent*, the *Barnsley Chronicle* and several others whose names have long disappeared. Their reporting of events, be they bizarre, macabre or murderous, has been both detailed and enthralling. No researcher would have such easy recourse to the past had they not reported in detail not only the events but the people involved in them, mundane or sensational. It would seem that nothing of note ever happened over the past couple of centuries without a reporter, clutching a pad and pencil, being on site to record the event for posterity. I am eternally grateful for their vigilance, their accuracy and the various libraries' foresight in keeping copies of this written record.

My thanks must also go to a number of authors and their works: *Armley Gaol 1864–1961* by Malcolm Wright, *Crime in Sheffield* and *The Sheffield Gang Wars* by J.P. Bean, *Witchcraft in Yorkshire* by Patricia Crowther, *Strange South Yorkshire* by David Clark, *Hangmen of England* by Brian Bailey, *The Art of Mystery & Detective Stories* by Peter Haining, *Diary of a Hangman* by John Ellis, *The Sheffield Hanged* by David Bentley, *Black Barnsley* by Ian Harley and *The Encyclopaedia of Executions* by John J. Eddleston.

My research on this book has taken me into some dark corners of the past and en route I have met some extremely nice people. These interested folk have pointed me in the right direction when I have wandered off course and have directed me towards stories and events I would never have uncovered without their invaluable help. My thanks to all.

Every attempt has been made to contact owners of copyright for images used in this book. If any omission has been made it is not deliberate and no offence was intended.

Lastly I must thank Maureen Yule for her love, support and expertise in helping to bring this book to fruition.

Please note: All pictures are from the author's collection, unless otherwise credited.

INTRODUCTION

Towards the end of 1910 the celebrated international cellist August Van Been wrote a letter to John Ellis, Britain's official executioner, requesting that he send him a piece of the rope used in the execution of Hawley Harvey Crippen. The reason for so morbid a request was not Crippen's notoriety, nor was it because the keepsake could be used to impress guests around the dinner table. It was simply that the cellist had made a number of poor investments over the preceding months and needed a talisman, a good luck charm if you like, something to help him achieve more success in the future. Such was the power of the infamous. To touch the clothing of those newly hanged or to take possession of something owned or used during their execution had long been believed to hold some kind of powerful magic.

The dawn of the twentieth century and with it a more educated populace had obviously done little to discredit the practice. But John Ellis, who served as executioner for twenty-three years and was involved in 203 executions, would never have been allowed to agree to the request. The rope was the property of the Home Office as were all other pieces of apparatus at his disposal. Had he complied he would have been removed from a post in which he took a great deal of pride, and that he would never have been prepared to risk. However, the public's interest in the darker side of human nature and their fascination with all things macabre was so strong that trafficking in items of this type had once been commonplace.

Just how this bizarre belief developed is not known, but certainly during the latter half of the eighteenth century a widespread interest in crime and all things criminal was tapped into by a variety of writers. Most were poorly paid and remained unrecognised, but they were responsible for the production of broadsheets sold on the day of a public execution at this time. These broadsheets related the tale of the condemned and where possible the final confession, though this was often more fiction than fact. This in turn led to the *Newgate Calendars* or *Annals* which reported in greater detail, and often more graphic prose, those crimes deemed to be unusual. These accounts were accompanied by lurid woodcuts, which the broadsheet producers could plagiarise as they saw fit. A huge commercial success, the *Calendars* sold in their thousands and led Newgate chaplain, the Revd John Villette, to produce a book in four volumes known as *The Malefactor's Register*. An expensive work relating the stories of some of this country's most violent crimes, it sold

well among the wealthy but proved beyond the reach of ordinary people. Publishers were quick to recognise this fact. In order to reach a wider audience, they employed a small army of writers whose task it was to produce a weekly penny issue of *Newgate Crimes*, an almost comic-book format where fact and fiction were often blurred; it attracted a wide readership. The 'penny dreadful' had been born.

By the mid-nineteenth century penny dreadfuls had been replaced by weekly serials, eight-page issues of sensational crime stories, well illustrated but often poorly written and produced by publishers whose sole intent was to sell copy, and lots of it. A similar number of writers remained in employment but whereas those who had worked a century earlier were adhering in some small measure to the truth, here the brief was almost the opposite. Those who created the stories of what became known as the 'penny bloods' were under instructions to create as much drama and bloodshed as they could legitimately get away with, regardless of the truth. It obviously worked because these publications were hugely successful, fuelling the public's ever-growing interest in the gruesome, often shocking and certainly repellent world of the murderer and all that murder entailed.

By 1869, when public executions were banned and the scaffold erected within the confines of the prison grounds, these same weekly editions were used to tell the story of the accused in much the same way as the eighteenth-century broadsheets, which had been sold to the waiting crowds gathered around a public gibbet. Such was the interest that if the crime was considered more than usually important, the print run was increased to match demand. Interest was generated by local newspapers, most of which would have reported the crime and subsequent court hearing almost verbatim. The public at large would often still arrive in their thousands outside the prison gate on the day of an execution. Drawn by the stories or by morbid curiosity, they would stand in silence as the clock chimed out the appointed hour, wait for the prison chaplain to post the notice or raise the black flag to signify that the sentence had been carried out, then slowly break up into smaller groups and begin to make their journey home again.

Throughout the Victorian period public interest in this dark and lurid aspect of life remained obdurate. No ᵤrprise then that fiction writers began to turn their attention to crime, in some instances taking as their lead the convoluted plots of the penny papers. Edgar Allan Poe, who had enjoyed success in America with his fictional detective, Auguste Dupin, found a market in England. George Reynolds, who had written for the penny bloods, found success with his books of crime stories and these men were followed by such greats as Wilkie Collins and Charles Dickens. The detective genre had been born.

To a public brought up on stories of the criminal fraternity this was manna from heaven. Eagerly they bought the books, keen to understand how the criminal mind worked – it mattered little whether the story was truth or fiction. All the book-buying public wanted to know was the how and why of a crime. What Poe, Collins and other authors of the late nineteenth century were able to bring to their readers was precisely that, plus a little extra. By this time the police force in Britain was reasonably well established. It lacked scientific knowledge but revelled in procedure, priding itself on the law's ability not only to catch those who perpetrated ghastly crimes, but also to try them effectively in a court of law. Authors of the stature of Collins and Dickens understood the mechanics of the police force. Dickens retained a fascination for police work for much of his life; he knew a number of Bow Street Runners and, as part of his own research, had spent time talking to convicts in Newgate prison. One of the leading policemen of his day,

Inspector Field, no doubt helped fill any gaps in his knowledge of how the force functioned. A great deal of this information was no doubt imparted to his friend Collins, who through a chance discovery of a copy of the *Newgate Calendar* also began to develop an interest in crime and criminals. When Sir Arthur Conan Doyle was thrown into the mix there is little wonder that Victorian readers were able to sustain their appetite for all that is grim.

But there were others who were beginning to explore areas that had proved taboo for previous generations. The Victorians not only wanted to know about murder, suicide, infanticide and execution, they also wanted to know what happened next. Did the spirit exist and if so in what form? Where did the spirit go after death? This led to the growth of spiritualism and a fascination with death itself. Newspapers, all too well aware of the reading public's foibles, began to detail the macabre side of life whenever the opportunity allowed. They reported on coroners' courts, funerals, murders and subsequent court hearings with greater detail than had hitherto been felt necessary. The public, through ever-increasing newspaper sales, were demanding ever-greater knowledge and there were reporters only too eager to give it to them. Stories of the condemned man's last moments were no longer enough. The readers of the local dailies wanted a reporter inside the prison sharing the last meal and helping the convicted on to the scaffold. And if that couldn't happen then a fictional account was perfectly acceptable – just as long as it sounded genuine. Right up to the last executions in mainland Britain, those of Peter Anthony Allen and John Robson Welby who were hanged on the same day in 1964, this continued to be the case.

Today, the interest has not waned. If it had, TV would not exist in its current form and writers would not sell books on all aspects of crime, be it fact or fiction. No one would know of the dark arts and 'paranormal' would simply be a hard word to pronounce.

This *Grim Almanac* is therefore a collection of many of these stories, some bizarre, some fascinating, some macabre but all equally absorbing. I have spent many hours researching those dark corners of South Yorkshire where witchcraft, body snatching, highway robbery, murder and execution, in whatever guise, have stalked through life. I have visited the dark side, plumbed the depths of past despair and peered over the rim of that dark and bottomless pit where demons lurk, with only a candle's light to see by . . . metaphorically speaking of course. I invite you to take the same journey and meet the people that populated the past . . . while I hold the candle at arm's length.

Police Inspector R. Parkinson (1915–25). *(Rotherham Archives and Local Studies)*

JANUARY

Old Toll Bar House.
(Rotherham Archives and Local Studies)

1 JANUARY **1810** Thomas Tuke, who had died just before Christmas, decreed in his will that a penny was to be given to every child that attended his funeral and a shilling to every woman living in Wath. He also requested that at noon every Christmas Day in perpetuity, forty dozen penny buns were to be thrown from Wath bell tower. Seven hundred children mourned his demise, filling the churchyard and lining his funeral route as the coffin passed. They all received their reward, as did the women, but the distribution of so many penny buns proved a bequest too far. It was abandoned several years after his death because an ever-increasing number of people suffered broken limbs in the scramble to catch the buns as they fell from the lofty height of the tower.

2 JANUARY **1676** Adam Hawksworth, innkeeper of Rotherham, appeared before the bench at Rotherham's courthouse charged with harbouring the notorious highwayman John Brace, alias William Nevison or, as he was known locally, Swift Nick. Nevison, who by this time was well known throughout Yorkshire, was captured weeks later having made a ride from Kent to York in fifteen hours. He was eventually imprisoned in the Yorkshire capital, but escaped after a five-year incarceration. Freedom was short. Recaptured in March 1684, he made the walk to the scaffold a few weeks later. As for Adam Hawksworth, magistrates ordered him to remove his sign, effectively stripping him of his livelihood.

3 JANUARY **1842** Williamson Etches was appointed police superintendent for Doncaster, as reported in the police register. He was to base himself in a room inside the town hall, which was to act as his temporary station house. Along with his salary of £80 per year he was given an allowance of coal for his fire and candles to light his office.

4 JANUARY **1880** Charles Beasley (aged 12) shot his friend Edward Shepherd in the head while they were playing near their school at Swinton. He had taken his father's gun from the house that morning believing it was not loaded. Over the course of a couple of hours the two lads had both used the weapon, pretending to shoot at each other, but had not actually pulled the trigger. That was left to Charles and only happened as a result of an accidental slip. After pointing the revolver at an old wooden door he stumbled as he aimed, pressed hard on the trigger and poor Edward was unfortunately in his line of fire as the gun went off.

5 JANUARY **1923** Lee Doon (aged 27), a Chinese laundry worker, was executed by Thomas Pierrepoint for the murder of his boss, Sing Lee, in Crookes, Sheffield. Doon had apparently planned to rob his employer and on Saturday 9 September had stayed behind after work for that sole purpose. In what was a frenzied attack, he beat and strangled the man then buried his body in the cellar. On the following morning Lily Siddall, who had worked at the laundry for eighteen months, turned up for work as usual and was told that Sing had returned to China. But Lily had got to know her boss rather well and found the idea that he would have returned to China without her knowledge hard to believe. Suspicious of the story of so unlikely a journey, she resolved to discover if there could have been any truth in it. Resourceful as ever, and aware of Sing's contacts in the North West, she travelled to Liverpool where she contacted his relatives and told them what she knew. They were equally disbelieving and told Lily that if he had returned to China it had been without their knowledge, which was highly unlikely. When she returned to the Sheffield laundry her worst fears were confirmed: after finding no one managing the shop, she discovered Doon digging in the cellar. Police were called, and the beaten body was discovered locked inside a trunk some 2ft down.

1842   After a previous falling-out Henry Vaughan stormed into the Sheffield home of Hannah, Sarah and Harriett Poole and attempted to shoot all three sisters. Whether the gun was faulty or his aim was off is not known, but his shots missed all three. Drawn by the women's screams of alarm, neighbours quickly gathered outside the house. Vaughan ignored their shouts to throw the gun out into the street, and instead turned it upon himself. This time his aim was true and the bullet penetrated his heart, killing him instantly.

6 JANUARY

1926   Lorraine Lax (aged 28), fond of drink and gambling, was executed for the murder of his wife Elizabeth. Having always had a stormy relationship, the couple had split up on two occasions over the previous five years, but by August of 1925 were living together again in Sheffield. On the morning of the 31st Lax claimed his wife had attacked him with a cut-throat razor and in the ensuing fight he had disarmed her and killed her in the heat of the moment. Unhelpfully for his case, an examination of Elizabeth's body revealed that a great deal of violence had been used during the killing. It was unlikely, argued the prosecution, that events were as claimed by the defendant. The jury agreed.

7 JANUARY

1657   On this day Thomas Jefferson and his wife Mary, of Woodhouse, Sheffield, were arraigned before the court charged with practising witchcraft. Both, it was claimed, had dug up bodies from Woodhouse churchyard for the purpose of necromancy. According to locals Thomas Jefferson had also cast a spell upon a young woman, Mary Almond, which had caused an illness from which she had died, while his wife had bewitched an old woman by the name of Beatrice Wynne. The court declared Thomas innocent, but hanged his wife as a witch.

8 JANUARY

1845   The statement of accounts from Sheffield's police showed the force was staffed by seventeen constables (first class) at a cost of 18s per week, seventeen constables (second class) at a cost of 17s per week and sixty-four night watchmen at varying rates of pay, all under the watchful eye of three sergeants at a weekly rate of 21s, three inspectors at 25s and a chief constable who cost the city £315 per year.

9 JANUARY

A dungeon and lock-up, similar to Sheffield's town gaol.

10 JANUARY   1840   Samuel Holberry, a stranger to Sheffield's streets, was arrested at his house in Eyre Lane after it became known that his arrival coincided with a planned Chartist uprising to attack and burn the city. At his home a quantity of spears, daggers, firearms, bombshells, hand grenades, ball cartridges and fireballs were discovered in a back room. The self-styled leader of an ill-disciplined group of rebels had planned the attack for the following morning but an unknown informer had tipped off the head of Sheffield's local yeomanry. As he was led away, a muster of this rabble army took place in the streets and surrounding lanes, resulting in shots being fired. A number of night watchmen were wounded before the army were able to break up the mob and regain control of the city. Holberry and his co-conspirator Thomas Booker were charged and tried for high treason two months later and

Drawing of halberds of the type discovered in Samuel Holberry's house.

sentenced to four and three years' imprisonment respectively, sentence to be served at York Castle where Holberry died two years into his sentence. Booker was released in August 1841.

1858 *The Rotherham and Masbrough Advertiser* reported that Sarah Ann Harman had pleaded guilty at the Sheffield Intermediate Sessions to stealing a gold watch, a handkerchief, a prayer book, a frock, three books, a brass measure and a pearl handle. In the interval between the robberies and her appearance before the bench, she had married. The court therefore decided upon a more lenient sentence believing marriage would lead her to a better course of life. She was imprisoned for one month.

11 JANUARY

1897 George Flowers, labourer, appeared before magistrates at Rotherham West Riding Police Court charged with arson. After being refused admission to Rotherham workhouse because he had been there so often, he had resolved to force police to arrest him in order to gain shelter for the night. Walking into fields at Hough, Rawmarsh, he had deliberately set light to hay ricks, then calmly walked the streets in search of a policeman to whom he could admit his guilt. However, Flowers rather ineptly caused far greater damage than he had intended and magistrates ordered him to be remanded and stand trial at the Spring Assizes.

12 JANUARY

1858 Four men died at Killamarsh pit when the rope securing the cage that lowered them to the coalface snapped. According to the coroner's inquest held at the Navigation Inn there had been a small fire the previous day and the rope had been burnt. George Twigg, responsible for ensuring the men's safety, ought to have adhered to the written rules as laid down by the government's inspector of mines. It transpired during the hearing, however, that the unfortunate George Twigg could neither read nor write.

13 JANUARY

1860 The tragic case of Hugh Connor, an Irishman living in Barnsley, was related at an inquest held this day. It appeared that Connor had been out drinking the night before with a good friend. Having consumed far too much alcohol, the two set out to return to their lodgings, a walk of some three-quarters of a mile. Caught up in a fierce storm and unable to continue walking against the wind, Connor fell into the gutter and was left there by his friend who could no longer support his weight. He was found dead next morning still lying beside the road but with his trousers round his ankles because his braces had frozen stiff and snapped.

14 JANUARY

1908 In their eagerness to see a cinematograph show at Barnsley's public hall, sixteen children between 4 and 6 years of age were crushed or suffocated to death on a staircase. Not realising just how many children had arrived at the hall, organisers stationed inside at the top of the stairs turned the leading children around and sent them back down, intending the group to enter the building on the ground floor. But such was the popularity of the show that

15 JANUARY

hundreds had joined the back of the queue, the sad result being that those caught in the middle had nowhere to go and died in the ensuing crush.

16 JANUARY   1865   A tragic event occurred on this day, when Mary Ann Morris (aged 8) lay down to sleep before a roaring fire. Hot cinders fell on to her clothes and ignited. By the time she awoke and became aware of her awful situation she was engulfed by fire. In a state of panic she ran all around the house screaming for help until neighbours rushed in and managed to extinguish the flames. But it was too late: Mary died some hours later.

17 JANUARY   1896   This date brought a report of a freak accident at Bentley. Reuben Clark, a young man of 20, was on his way to work when he saw a loose horse running down the street towards him. Clark had worked with horses in the past and he stepped out into the centre of the road waving his arms in the air to slow the horse down. As it reached him he grabbed at the reins, but just as he managed to turn the horse's head it reared, he slipped and the frightened animal brought the full weight of its front legs down upon his neck. He was killed instantly.

18 JANUARY   1681   At the Angel Inn, Doncaster, Scottish nobleman Alexander, Earl of Eglington, and a travelling companion named Thomas Maddox played dice. After a sizeable win the Earl demanded Maddox pay his debt. Maddox refused, a fight of sorts ensued and, drawing his sword, the Earl stabbed Maddox twice. When Maddox died of his wounds, the Earl Alexander was charged with his murder. At his subsequent trial he was found not guilty and the case was dismissed.

19 JANUARY   **Old Yorkshire Beliefs, Omens and Sayings**
If a loud, mysterious tap is heard as of a bullet falling on a table, or three successive strokes on the chamber floor or any of the doors, the hearer is either doomed to die or to hear of the death of a near and dear friend.

To see a pigeon alight on the roof is an omen of sickness about to befall the family.

20 JANUARY   1911   The trial of William Hammond, a miner of Wosbro' Dale accused of murdering his father of the same name, opened this day. But although he was found guilty and sentenced to hang, public opinion and a petition of 3,000 signatures had the sentence commuted to one of life imprisonment.

21 JANUARY   1859   Sitting magistrates at Barnsley Courthouse found George Acklam guilty of neglecting his family on this day. After leaving his wife and child five years earlier in order to travel to America, from where he sent no money home, he had returned to Barnsley claiming his wife to be a drunkard and demanding the child be given into his custody. The court disagreed, citing his failure to support his family financially, and insisted he not only repay the amount of relief given to his wife during his absence, but also pay court costs.

A seventeenth-century woodcut of a woman baking bread to be used as a cure for whooping cough.

South Yorkshire Cures

To cure whooping cough you must eat bread baked only by a woman who married without changing her name.

22 JANUARY

1823   The government introduced the treadmill into the house of correction for the first time. This was a piece of equipment that served no useful purpose other than as a form of punishment. Prisoners sent to the treadmill would walk up its moving platform for 6 hours a day and climb the equivalent of 8,640ft, while existing on a diet of oatmeal, bread and water.

23 JANUARY

1870   Riots broke out in the early hours of the morning at Westwood, Thorncliffe, after employers Messrs Newton Chambers & Co., owners of the Thorncliffe Colliery, gave their entire workforce one month's notice to quit their jobs and their homes. During a strike lasting seventy-three weeks the company consistently refused to recognise the trade union and workers stubbornly refused to return to work. After the company attempted to renegotiate contracts with each individual miner and to replace the strikers with new labour, over 300 colliers gathered at Tankersley Park to voice their opposition. Local police officers, armed with cutlasses, were sent on to the streets to break up the meeting. When the miners refused to disperse, the

24 JANUARY

A trade union meeting like that which took place at Tankersley Park.

police were ordered to charge the crowd, which they did, causing numerous casualties. After regrouping at dawn around Tankersley pit, the miners, whose numbers had swelled to over 500, attacked the homes of company directors and were only prevented from inflicting serious damage by the arrival of police reinforcements who formed a line and charged into the rioters. A pitched battle then broke out, and it was some time before police regained control of the streets. Twenty-three men were consequently arrested and sent for trial at York.

1850 The Association for the Prosecution of Felons was formed in Sheffield. Supported by the moneyed classes, it was intended to provide money to be used to fund prosecution cases against petty thieves, particularly among travellers who arrived in the city with the winter fair.

1835 The medical school at the corner of Eyre Street and Charles Lane in Sheffield was attacked by a mob after a woman was found lying in the street outside, screaming murder. The crowd believed she had been 'burked' and taken into the school for intended dissection. The term had entered common parlance after it became known that the notorious Edinburgh body-snatchers Burke and Hare had often selected their victims at random from among the public, and suffocated them in order to provide corpses for medical dissection. In this instance, however, the woman had merely had a row with her husband, a caretaker at the medical school, which ended in her being thrown out into the street. Regrettably this information was not relayed to the rampaging crowd until the school had been set alight, by which time it was too late to save the building.

1859 William Wilson, a brass turner of Sheffield, was murdered outside the post office at Hartshead. According to a report in the *Barnsley Chronicle* he was attacked by four men, one of whom stabbed him in the abdomen, and left him for dead in the gutter. Passers-by believed Wilson to be drunk and it was some considerable time before they answered his shouts for help, a delay that surely helped shorten his life. Eventually he was carried into the town hall where he lay for several hours while men went in search of a doctor. It was subsequently discovered that 4ft of the man's intestines had been dislodged by the knife wound and were being held in by his shirt. When local surgeon William Booth had finally been located and brought to the hall there was little hope of recovery and he died several hours after the operation to save his life. No one was ever caught for the attack.

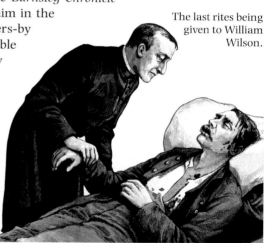

The last rites being given to William Wilson.

1860 The remarkable funeral of Henry Walker took place on this day at Masbrough Chapel Yard. The family ironworks had been responsible for the manufacture of most of the cannon fired during the American War of Independence and a large proportion of the ordnance used during the Napoleonic Wars, and had cast the iron bridges of Sunderland, Yarm, Staines and Southwark. As a mark of respect all the shops in Rotherham closed at eleven o'clock in the morning while the great bell of the parish church tolled in solemn recognition of the sad event. Borne to the family tomb encased in a lead coffin, the body was carried in a hearse drawn by four black horses and followed by four mourning coaches and several

Henry Walker whose powerful family owned the Rotherham ironworks.
(Rotherham Archives and Local Studies)

other private carriages. The funeral cortège left Clifton Hall and formed a lengthy procession as it wound its way down Doncaster Gate, along College Street, Bridgegate and into College Road. Here it stopped briefly to be joined by the Revd Vaughan, deacons of the chapel and students of Rotherham College before continuing its journey to Masbrough. Hundreds lined the streets to mourn the passing of the head of one of Rotherham's greatest families whose wealth and prestige had been created by the building of the vast ironworks in the Holmes area a century before. Later they stood in silence as the coffin, draped in black, was lowered into the family tomb.

Unveil thy bosom faithful tomb,
Take this new treasure to thy trust,
And give these sacred relics room
Awhile, to slumber in the dust.

29 JANUARY   1836   Rules of Sheffield's Scotland Street Prison (extract from prison report, which claimed prisoners made up their own rules).

At the coming in of any bird (prisoner) he shall pay *2s 6d* to the garnish master, or have his hat and coat taken for security, and if not paid in seven days, the coals of the room will be stopped until it is paid. But should any bird go out under twelve hours he will have *1s 3d* returned; and at the coming in of a woman, she shall pay *1s 3d* garnish, or have her bonnet and shawl taken for security until the same is paid. At the coming in of a bird a captain or substitute will attend, or be fined *2s* for neglect of duty. Any man coming in shall commence nancy next morning at nine o'clock.

30 JANUARY   1902   A court at Barnsley declared Lily Shaw of Birdwell to have been insane when, in a fit of depression, she hurled her infant son into the reservoir at Elsecar where he drowned.

31 JANUARY   1905   Seven people, including 15-year-old twin brothers, died on this day when the Scotch express hit a mail train on the Midland Railway at Storrs Mill, Cudworth, in heavy fog after a breakdown in communication between the engine and the various signal boxes. The grieving families were eventually paid a share of £20,000 compensation.

FEBRUARY

PC23 William George Winks, *c.* 1900.
(Rotherham Archives and Local Studies)

1 FEBRUARY 1865 A report appeared of a distressing double murder in Sheffield. The bodies of two newborn babies, a girl and a boy, were discovered at 11 a.m. by a man named Thomas Rawson as he emptied an ash pit. Both had been strangled to death with a piece of ribbon. The bodies were placed in a bath and the boy revived briefly, but then died. Investigations were made but police were not hopeful of making an arrest.

2 FEBRUARY 1838 An inquest opened into the death of William Teal (aged 11), who had been walking alongside a cart loaded with coal. As it passed through Mexborough he lost his footing and slipped into the road, where one of the rear wheels ran over his head, killing him instantly.

3 FEBRUARY 1635 Curiosity got the better of 12-year-old Joshua Bradley of Hexthorpe when he saw a piece of shirt floating in the River Don near Doncaster. After gently poking it with a stick and discovering it was wrapped around something soft he cautiously pulled it back towards the riverbank where he hauled it back on to dry land. Intrigued, he proceeded to roll it over several times and after a few more investigatory pokes and prods decided that it was the sleeve of a white shirt, knotted at both ends and containing something heavy. Warily he slowly drew open one of the knots, tipped the sleeve on its end and then stared in total disbelief as the dead body of a newborn baby girl rolled out and across his feet.

4 FEBRUARY 1860 This day brought a report of the inquest at the Albion Inn, Barnsley, into the death of 8-year-old Edward Moore. Neighbours gave evidence that they heard an argument break out in the Moore house at around one o'clock in the morning and clearly heard Edward shout out, 'Father, Father do forgive me. I'll never do it any more,' followed by shrieks, screams and the sound of someone being dragged down the stairs and into the cellar. Doctor Wainwright, who had carried out the post-mortem, told the jury that the young boy had sustained a 5in fracture of his skull, such as would have occurred had he been thrown from room to room, but that though the fracture was the cause of death, that death had not been instantaneous. In fact the unfortunate child had lived for several days. Numerous witnesses testified to the fact that they had seen the boy during the week following the attack made on him by his father, Thomas, but that the youngster had clearly been ill. The jury, after listening to evidence that the assault was probably caused through drink and that Edward had not been the subject of frequent beatings, returned a verdict of manslaughter.

5 FEBRUARY 1906 In what was dubbed the Melton Hall Mystery by local newspapers, under-footman George Percy Finn (aged 18) appeared in court charged with the theft of a tiara from Mrs Montagu of Melton Hall. A wedding gift from Frederick Montagu to his new wife, it consisted of 1,300 diamonds, some of great size and brilliance. The tiara was kept in a plate-safe in the footman's pantry and throughout January its theft had triggered a countrywide search

for the thief. It took three weeks to uncover the under-footman as the perpetrator and then only after he had made a vital mistake in his plan. Finn had never intended to keep the tiara; he wanted to ransom it for £500. Three days after its disappearance a letter arrived at the house addressed to Mr Montagu. In it was the ransom demand and an instruction. If the Montagus wanted their property back they were to place an advertisement in the advertising columns of the *Daily Mail* using only the letters 'XYZ'. After consultation with Doncaster's Police Superintendent Hicks it was decided to comply. This brought a second letter detailing in what denomination the ransom was to be paid and how. At

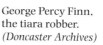

George Percy Finn, the tiara robber.
(*Doncaster Archives*)

The three policemen who captured George Finn.
(*Doncaster Archives*)

The 1st and 3rd footmen questioned by police.
(*Doncaster Archives*)

Superintendent Hicks who arrested Finn.
(*Doncaster Archives*)

that juncture the policeman noticed that both letters had a London postmark. Moreover, once a brief history of every member of the Hall's household was obtained, it transpired that only Finn had a London connection. When he had applied for his job he had stated that not only had he worked in the city but that his mother still lived there. A train journey to the capital revealed that Finn's mother had also received two sealed letters from her son requesting that she simply post them on, which she had done. The under-footman was immediately arrested and confessed everything. The tiara, he told police, was buried in the garden border. It was found within hours and George Finn pleaded guilty at Doncaster's courthouse.

1858 An explosion was reported in Sheffield. At a house in Scotland Street three people were killed when the upper storey of a two-storey house owned by John Corbridge exploded. Such was the intensity of the blast that it completely destroyed the whole of the upper level, which then fell in upon the ground floor. A Mr Bywater, who rented the upstairs rooms, had used them as a fireworks factory. Having been given notice a week earlier by John Corbridge

6 FEBRUARY

because of concerns over safety, he had been killed outright by the blast, as had Corbridge's wife and sister-in-law who had been about to sit down to Saturday lunch when the explosion took place, trapping them inside their own kitchen where they burned to death.

7 FEBRUARY   **1792**   Notorious highwayman Spence Broughton was condemned to death for the robbery of the Sheffield to Rotherham mail. Born in Lincolnshire to wealthy parents, 26-year-old Broughton had been given a farm by his father at the age of 22 and had eventually married into another wealthy farming family, his wife bringing even greater riches as part of her dowry. Lamentably for her and his own family Broughton managed to spend most of the money over four years on gambling and drink, and almost nothing on his farming business. Eventually thrown out, he first travelled to London where he set up in lodgings with a Mrs Hill, fell in with bad company and began to lead a life of crime. The opportunity of robbing the mail brought him to Rotherham and, in company with an accomplice named Oxley, he lay in wait on the Rotherham road where he held up the mail delivery and stole a number of valuable letters,

Spence Broughton, the highwayman. *(Sheffield Libraries, Archives and Local Studies)*

Opposite: Spence Broughton's last letter. *(Sheffield Libraries, Archives and Local Studies)*

The following moſt pathetic and affecting Letter was written by Spence Broughton, to his wife, the night before his Execution.

York Caſtle, April 14, 1792.

My Dear Eliza

THIS is the laſt affectionate token thou wilt ever receive from my hand:---an hand that trembles at my approaching diſſolution; ſo ſoon---ſo very ſoon to enſue.

Before thou wilt open this laſt epiſtle of thine unfortunate huſband, theſe eyes, which overflow with tears of contrition, ſhall have ceaſed to weep, and this heart now fluttering on the verge of eternity, ſhall beat no more.

I have prepared my mind to meet death without horror; and how happy, had that death been the common viſitation of nature. Be not diſcomforted. God will be your friend. In the ſolitude of my cell I have ſought nim. His ſpirit hath ſupported me---hath aſſiſted me in my prayers, and many a time, in the moment of remorſeful anguiſh hath whiſpered peace: for, my dear Eliza, I never added cruelty to injuſtice.

Yet, tho' I have reſolved to meet death without fear, one part of my awful ſentence ---a ſentence aggravated by being merited---fills me with horror: When I reflect that my poor remains, the tokens of mortality, muſt not ſleep in peace, but be buffetted by the ſtorms of heaven, or parched by the ſummers ſun, while the traveller ſhrinks from them with diſguſt and terror, this conſideration freezes my blood. This cell---this awful gloom---theſe irons---yea death is not ſo grievous. Why will the laws continue to ſport with the wretched after life is at an end?

My Eliza!---my friend!--- my wife!---the laſt ſad ſcene approaches, when I ſhall be no more. When I ſhall leave the world, and thee, my dear to its mercy:---not only thee but my unprotected children, the pledges of a love, through misfortune, through diſſipation, through vice and infamy, on my part, unchanged. Ah! fool that I was, to think FRIENDSHIP could exiſt but with VIRTUE! Had I liſtened to the advice thou haſt ſo often given me, we had been a happy family, reſpectable, and reſpected. But it is paſt. That advice hath been ſlighted. I am doomed to an ignominious death, and thou and my children, horrid thought! to infamy. To thee alone I truſt the education of thoſe ill-fated creatures, whom I now more than ever love, and weep for. Warn them to avoid GAMING of every deſcription; that baneful vice which has cauſed their father to be ſuſpended a long and laſting ſpectacle, to feed the eye of curioſity: Teach them the ways of RELIGION in their early years. 'Cauſe them to learn ſome trade, that buſineſs may fill their minds and leave no room for diſſipation. When ſeated round your winter's fire, when the little innocents enquire after their unfortunate father, ah! tell them GAMING was his ruin:---he neglected all religious duties---he never converſed with his heart in ſolitude---he ſtifled the upbraidings of conſcience, in the company of the lewd and profligate, and is hung on high a ſad and diſmal warning to after times. I ſee thee thus employed, while the tears trickle down that dear face which I have ſo ill deſerved.

Adieu my Eliza!---adieu for ever! The morning appears for the laſt time to theſe ſad eyes. Pleaſant would death be to me on a ſick bed, after my ſoul had made her peace with God. With God I hope her peace is made.---He is not a God all terror, but a God of mercy: on that mercy I rely, and on the interpoſition of a Saviour. May my tears, my penitence, and deep contrition, be acceptable to that Almighty Being, before whom I am ſhortly to appear.

Once more Eliza, adieu for ever. The pen falls from my hand and ſlumbers overtake me. The next will be the ſleep of death.

SPENCE BROUGHTON.

including one intended for the powerful Walker family. This important letter contained a French bill of exchange for a considerable sum payable to Joseph Walker. Broughton sent this to London with forged signatures and had it exchanged for cash. It brought with it his downfall, arrest and inevitable trial in York. Guilty of highway robbery, he was executed at Tyburn, and his body gibbeted and hung in irons at the corner of Clifton Street where it remained for the next thirty-five years.

8 February **1865** A report was published about a Sheffield man named McHugh who travelled to Birkenhead with three packing cases, all labelled 'Eggs'. Leaving them at the port he gave instructions that they were to be transported to Ireland and would be collected. After a few days suspicions were aroused by a bad smell from one of the three cases. Unsure whether the smell was just bad eggs or something more sinister, officials called the police. They prised it open and found inside, wrapped in straw, a coffin. Inside the coffin was the badly decomposed body of a woman. McHugh was quickly traced and taken back to the port where he identified the body as being that of his wife. A full examination revealed that the woman had died of natural causes. McHugh told police she was to be buried in Ireland but that the only packing cases he had to transport her body had all been labelled 'Eggs'.

9 February **Old Yorkshire Beliefs, Omens and Sayings**
A flock of geese flying over the house portends a death. If the flock flies to the side then someone close will suffer illness.

10 February **1937** Andrew Bagley (aged 62), alias William Smith, was executed for the brutal murder of 16-year-old Irene Hart in her own home. The case had gained enormous notoriety after her body had been discovered by her stepmother, shut up inside a trunk once used to store Irene's childhood toys, and hidden away in a bedroom cupboard. Known famously as the Tin Trunk Murder, it caused police across England to coordinate in one of the largest manhunts in their history and created headlines in the national press, though it did not result in Bagley's arrest. Police had to wait for six weeks before he was finally caught in a library on the outskirts of Nottingham. He never confessed to the murder but did tell the jury at his trial that he had been in the house on the day Irene died, insisting that he had hidden in the front room when Irene had a visitor, a man he knew only as Tom. But subsequent enquiries proved Tom to be no more than a figment of Bagley's imagination. Police, forensic science and a number of neighbours were able to prove that no one other than Andrew Bagley had been in the house on the day Irene was murdered. Their evidence condemned him to the gallows.

11 February **1922** George Harry Robinson, a Mexborough miner, was sentenced to death for the murder of his wife Edith. He had cut her throat with his own razor and then made a failed suicide bid. The sentence was later commuted to life imprisonment.

1803 Colonel Despard and six others were executed for inciting rebellion in Barnsley. Arrested after a secret meeting at Carr Green in Barnsley, he was found guilty at his trial in London. Thirty-four years later, in 1837, while developing land around Clayton West just north of Barnsley, a man named William Crossley discovered a hoard of weapons, mainly spears, believed to have been part of Despard's intended arsenal.

12 FEBRUARY

1865 The *Doncaster Chronicle* reported on a wretched-looking creature: Mary Huntingdon was brought up for the twenty-fifth time before the Rotherham Police Court for being drunk and riotous. Released from prison only one week earlier, she was arrested in Masbrough for the same offence. The bench committed her to three months' imprisonment but Mary, taking great offence at their decision, attempted to hurl her shoes at them and had to be forcibly restrained by officers and carried, shouting and swearing, to the cells. She made a reappearance later the same day for smashing all the cell windows and her water jug. The bench added a fine to their earlier sentence and she threatened that on her release she would attack their homes.

13 FEBRUARY

1913 Harry Turner (aged 15) appeared before magistrates with a badly bruised face and black eye, charged with striking his pony several times and then hanging on to its tail. The bruises were part of the price he had paid when the horse, who did not take too kindly to being mistreated in this way, retaliated and almost kicked him to death. The other part of the price was a 15s fine for cruelty.

14 FEBRUARY

1836 On this day Doncaster appointed four night watchmen, at 12s per week and one day watchman at 18s per week. According to police records, within one month of these appointments two of the night watchmen had been suspended for carrying out unlawful arrests and drinking while on duty.

15 FEBRUARY

1828 Reported on this day was the inquest at the Crown Inn, Bawtry, into the murder of John Dyon, whose body was found beside the gate that led on to his land at Brancroft, near Doncaster. He had been shot once through the left side of his body, the ball entering his chest and probably killing him instantly. Forty-year-old Dyon, married with three daughters and living with an aged father,

16 FEBRUARY

had spent the day at Doncaster market. After a fruitful afternoon he had ridden to Brancroft with a friend, the two parting company at the gate at around 8 p.m. According to his wife's testimony, when he had not returned to the farmhouse by midnight she organised the search that subsequently discovered his body at a little after 2 a.m. A severe frost had settled about his clothes and he was badly frozen. Nothing had been stolen: his watch was still in his pocket, as was £41 in cash. The coroner returned the inevitable verdict of wilful murder and within days of the hearing, brother William Dyon and William's son John had been arrested. Both men had been seen near the murder site earlier on the day of the shooting, and police discovered that they had retrieved guns from a nearby barn. William was known to have harboured a grudge against his brother, jealous of the attention paid to him by their father and angry that of the two it had been John who had received the lion's share of land, property and money. Both were eventually tried for murder and found guilty. Just who had fired the fatal shot was never known and a crowd of over 10,000 onlookers who had turned out to watch the double drop did not really care – though John was later reported as having confessed his involvement moments before his death. Not so his father, who had refused throughout to acknowledge his guilt and had shouted out at his son as the two stood on the scaffold, imploring him to remain silent.

17 FEBRUARY **1791** John Minitor, in an act of wanton vandalism, set fire to a barn at Whiston, destroying the building and everything inside it. No reason was given for the arson but it was believed to have been carried out because Minitor had been sacked from his job tending cattle. He had threatened revenge for his sacking and of course the barn had been an easy target. He was quickly arrested and at the Summer Assizes he was found guilty. The sentence was death.

18 FEBRUARY **1859** Rotherham woman Esther Griggs was in court in London, charged with throwing her baby out of the bedroom window while drunk. The woman, who cried loudly throughout, also fainted twice while in the dock and had to be helped to remain standing as the court heard the case. The defence pleaded with the court to accept that the woman had been in a state of temporary insanity at the time, but the judge refused to accept the argument, sending her to trial.

19 FEBRUARY **1858** Highway robbery at Elsecar was reported in the *Rotherham and Masbrough Advertiser*. Richard Saville of Chapeltown was found beneath the wheels of his own gig, badly beaten, at 3 a.m. After spending the previous day in Barnsley he had begun his journey home in the early evening, stopping off at the Stafford Arms at Hoyland. Here he had stayed for some time, playing a series of games, all for money, with a number of regulars. Investigations revealed that hardly a man in the pub that night had not been aware of just how much money Saville was carrying. After watching his antics at the bar, insisting on buying drinks for his new-found friends

and accepting almost any kind of gamble anyone cared to make, most described his demeanour as careless. It was after 11 p.m. before he could be persuaded to leave and, somewhat the worse for wear, drive himself home. At Elsecar he was ambushed by four men, quite probably some of those who had watched his performance at the public house in Hoyland and who intended to make him pay for his public exuberance. They dragged him to the ground, beat him about the head, took what money they could find and left him for dead in the road. According to the doctor called to his assistance, his wounds were not as serious as they could have been and after leeches had been applied his recovery was reported as being slow but with good prospects of success.

Broom Road, Rotherham, *c.* 1900. *(Rotherham Archives and Local Studies)*

1880 On this day there was a fatal accident at Silkstone Colliery. What should have been a perfectly normal day for the Horne family turned to tragedy when a large piece of coal about 3yd long and 2yd wide fell from the roof of the shaft being worked by 61-year-old Edward Horne and his sons James (aged 18) and Herbert (aged 16). All three were killed instantly. The third son had a lucky escape. Scheduled to be working with his father and brothers, he had been summoned to appear before Barnsley magistrates that same day on a charge of obstructing a footpath. This saved his life.

20 FEBRUARY

21 FEBRUARY

Newspaper article on the murder of John Coe. (Rotherham Advertiser)

1880　An inquest into the murder of John Coe, whose body had been discovered in a field at Canklow, reported that he had been battered to death with a fence post, his injuries having been so severe that not only had the skull been fractured but the brain had been exposed. Police had already established that the victim had been drinking heavily in Whiston village and later in several pubs in Rotherham's town centre in the company of one John Wood. They also knew the only item of note missing from his body was a silver Geneva pocket-watch and a silver chain. Diligent police work eventually placed this same John Wood at a house in Wellgate where he had apparently taken Coe shortly before his death. A cab driver waiting for his fare outside a gentlemen's club then saw the two in company at around midnight, both walking in the direction of the murder site. The final nail, so to speak, came after witnesses stepped forward to say that Wood had appeared at the Stag Inn public house on the morning after the killing, wearing a pocket-watch of almost identical description – the same watch he had later that day given away to a man named Robert Poynter. Police found the man but not the watch. After reading of the murder Poynter told police he had returned the watch to Wood because he believed it to be the one stolen from John Coe. The watch was never found but there was enough evidence to arrest John Wood. Found guilty of murder, he was executed two months later.

22 FEBRUARY

1852　The shocking death of 22-year-old Charles Brookfield was reported by the *Barnsley Chronicle*. Employed by Morton's Corn Mill on the outskirts of the town, Mr Brookfield had died horrifically as the result of his efforts to free a piece of sacking from the mill's working mechanism. As he attempted to pull the sacking out from the machinery Brookfield was caught and dragged into the centre of the machine, which was spinning at 120 revolutions a minute. It took a few minutes before colleagues realised what had happened, and by the time they had managed to stop the machine, he had been literally torn apart.

SHOCKING
MURDER
AT ROTHERHAM.
APPREHENSION OF THE SUPPOSED MURDERER.
OTHERS SUSPECTED.
THE PRISONER BEFORE A MAGISTRATE.
OPENING OF THE INQUEST.

The neighbourhood of Rotherham has been so long free from crimes of intentional violence attended by fatal consequences, that the announcement on Thursday morning of the perpetration of a brutal murder in the outskirts of the town naturally gave rise to intense and widespread excitement. So shocking were the circumstances under which the victim was "done to death," that in many instances people were inclined to altogether discredit the narrative, and during the morning the Court House was besieged with hundreds of persons anxious to obtain reliable information. The sensation was greatly intensified by the apprehension and incarceration of a man on a charge of being concerned in the murder, and although outsiders could of course see and hear nothing that was passing within the police office or cells, the precincts of the Court House were thronged for hours with crowds eager to glean any scrap of news on the subject, from whatever source it came; and until late in the evening the College yard was never without groups of persons engaged in discussing the all-absorbing topic. Throughout yesterday, also, there were similar demonstrations of public feeling on the matter, large numbers of people congregating in front of the Court House debating the "pros and cons" of the case.

As will be gathered from the full details which follow, the murder was one of a terribly brutal character, but the exact circumstances under which it was committed, as well as the motive for the crime, are at present involved in mystery. The bare facts may be very briefly stated. Soon after eight o'clock on Thursday morning, the corpse of a man was found in a field bordering upon Canklow road. Although life was extinct, the body was quite warm. Death had been caused by fracture of the skull, the head of the deceased having been shockingly smashed—no other word affords an adequate description—the weapon of offence having been a heavy hedgestake, which was found, broken into two pieces, close by. On inquiry, it was found that the body was that of John Coe, a young man who had been employed as a farm labourer at Brinsworth, an agricultural hamlet about two miles from Rotherham. The deceased had been following Lord Fitzwilliam's hounds on foot on Wednesday, and had left the village of Whiston at eight o'clock on Wednesday night, presumably for home, along with his uncle, David Coe, a farm labourer, and also, it is believed, with another man. Immediately after the discovery of the body, certain matters transpired which led to suspicion falling on the uncle, who had been seen on the road leading from Canklow Wood to Brinsworth. He was at once followed by Police-sergeant Morley, and apprehended. At that time there were stains on his boots and clothing which were supposed to be those of blood, and on his boots was some chaff similar to that which lay on the ground where the corpse was found. When he was taken into custody he was in an advanced state of intoxication, but he nevertheless appeared to thoroughly understand the gravity of the charge preferred against him, and strenuously protested his innocence.
The searching inquiries instituted by Mr. Superintendent Gillett and his subordinates have elicited the fact that on Wednesday night the deceased had both money and a watch in his possession. On the body being searched after death, neither money nor watch were forthcoming. Whether the deceased himself got rid of them during the night, or whether he was robbed of them, remains to be proved. On Thursday evening, suspicion fell on a man named John Henry Wood, alias Greaves, of Whiston, who had been in company with the deceased along with other men.

1895 Brothers Henry (aged 12) and John Williams (aged 9) were drowned on this day after falling through ice on a Barnsley canal. Uriah Green, who had seen the tragedy and attempted to save the two boys, was also killed.

23 FEBRUARY

Rotherham policeman, 1910. *(Rotherham Archives and Local Studies)*

24 FEBRUARY   **1741**   Sarah Knowlin of Doncaster pleaded guilty at the magistrates' court to the theft of a shirt (value 10*d*) from her neighbour, Barbara Booth. The court sentenced her to be publicly whipped.

25 FEBRUARY   **1879**   Sheffield's most notorious criminal, a consummate and successful burglar, master of disguise and murderer, finally ended his life on the scaffold after being convicted of two murders. Born in 1832 Charles Peace had begun his life somewhat differently, working alongside his father as a lion-tamer until the age of 14. Possibly bored with the constant moving around or simply realising there was more money to be earned in industry, he took his leave of the family at around that age to work in a Sheffield steel mill. Here he would possibly have stayed had it not been for an accident that incapacitated him, forcing him out of work for two years. A long recuperation period followed, during which he learned to play the violin, but his circumstances throughout imposed severe financial restraints on him; money was in short supply, as was any means of earning it legitimately. He perhaps inevitably turned to crime, finding himself more in prison than out of it for the next thirty years until 1876. This year marked a crucial change of direction in his criminal activities. Petty theft gave way to murder when he shot and killed neighbour Arthur Dyson after an altercation at his house at Banner Cross in Sheffield. Married by this time, Peace sought shelter with his family in Hull for a few weeks before embarking on a burglary spree that would take him to Bristol, Bath, Birmingham and Nottingham, where he met up with Susan Bailey, a single woman of 35. The pair set up home together, regularly travelling into Sheffield to carry out robberies, before deciding to move back to Hull. Here, Peace was able to live a double life, splitting his time between the two women, his wife never aware of Susan Bailey, always believing that her husband was simply on the run from police for the burglary.

But Peace liked to live life on the edge, evidenced by his dangerous, though cleverly calculated, decision to move with Bailey into the house of a police sergeant where the couple, under the alias of Mr and Mrs Thompson, took lodgings. Offering his profession as a travelling dealer, Peace managed to carry out a number of incredibly successful robberies, always bringing the proceeds of his crimes back to the house before selling them on. As the burglaries became more audacious, however, so the police interest in his activities increased, forcing the pair to move to London. There the two were obliged constantly to change their address, moving around the capital to avoid capture until, in around 1877, Peace carried out a number of robberies that changed his financial position significantly. Reasonably wealthy, albeit on the proceeds of crime, he took out a lease on a large house in Peckham and, leaving Bailey behind, brought his wife and stepson to London. Intending to foster good relationships among the moneyed classes where family meant status, he changed his appearance, cut back his hair, stained his face with walnut juice and began to attend church – a veritable paragon of virtue and respectability.

THE NOTORIOUS BLACKHEATH BURGLAR.

PEACE,

THE MURDERER OF Mr. ARTHUR DYSON, Civil Engineer, Banner Cross,
Sheffield, November, 1876.

COPYRIGHT. TAKEN FROM LIFE.

Wanted poster
for Charles Peace.
(*Sheffield Libraries,
Archives and Local
Studies*)

But Peace was still unable to leave his criminal past behind him and, as if compelled, he continued to carry out burglaries across London, many of them very lucrative, until his eventual arrest at Blackheath. Here police trapped him outside a house as he left, and in the resultant struggle Peace shot a constable in the arm. At the police station, he gave his name as John Ward, which was not disputed. Eventually, found guilty of attempted murder, he was sentenced to life by an Old Bailey judge. There, in an almost bizarre fashion, it would have ended, with police never realising just who they had imprisoned – that is, had not the walnut juice begun to lose its staining effect on Peace's face, and had not Susan Bailey claimed a £100 reward for informing police that John Ward was in fact none other than Charles Peace.

26 February 1865 Mary Dunnell, a domestic servant at a house in Ravenfield, appeared before the Rotherham bench charged with having attempted to commit suicide. The court was told that she had purchased a quantity of laudanum after being jilted by her lover. Distraught at the sudden loss, she drank the lot, intent on killing herself. Fortunately or otherwise she was found by her employers within minutes of swallowing the bottle's contents and the arrival of Ravenfield's local surgeon saved her life. Whether remorseful or not Mary stood in the dock and wept bitterly throughout the proceedings, but there was little by way of compassion from the judges who sent her to prison for one week.

27 February **South Yorkshire Cures**
To cure bronchitis, go into a field in the early morning and dig a hole in the ground wide enough for a face. Lie down, place your face in the hole and breathe in freshly turned soil.

28 February 1859 A report was published on the inquest held at Barnsley into the death of Albert Greaves, a child of about 2 years old. It appeared that some months previously, the child fell into the cellar of his local grocery shop and injured his head. Unconscious for some fifteen minutes, he made a good recovery and was taken home by a neighbour. But unbeknown to anyone, the injury was far more serious than at first believed. His family had begun to notice something strange about him for a fortnight before he became seriously ill. According to the doctor who attended the child there was nothing that could have been done to save his life. The coroner returned a verdict of accidental death.

29 February 1865 Joseph Hughes of Barnsley appeared before magistrates at the Barnsley Courthouse on a charge of highway robbery. It was claimed that he had stopped John Fretwell at Wortley and robbed him of two shirts and a pocket handkerchief. Magistrates remanded him until the next Assize Court.

MARCH

Rotherham Town Hall and stocks, 1700.
(Rotherham Archives and Local Studies)

1 MARCH   **1832**   Reports of cholera in London reached South Yorkshire by letter and in the newspapers. Over the rest of the year 31,376 people across the country died of the disease, including over 400 in Sheffield.

2 MARCH   **1774**   A large crowd gathered in Sheffield's Fargate to protest against the price of coal, which many felt had become too expensive for most people to afford. Throughout the day as news of the protest spread, the numbers swelled, until thousands had spilled on to the streets to voice their protest. A riot ensued, with local constables being called out as the protesters began breaking windows. The crowd numbers were too great for the police to deal with, however. The army eventually arrived and fired several volleys above the rioters' heads in an attempt to disperse them. When that failed, shots were fired into the mass of rioters and a man by the name of Shaw was unfortunately killed. It was late evening before the authorities were able to regain control of the streets.

3 MARCH   **1865**   Solomon Stanton (aged 21), labourer, stood in the dock accused of the murder of his grandmother, Eliza Drabble, at Chapeltown. Four weeks earlier he had kicked her to death outside the Coach and Horses public house, the attack being only one of a series that he had made against her during the course of a couple of hours. Eliza, who had brought him up since he was a small child, had developed a habit of bringing him home from the pub whenever she thought he had had enough to drink. On this occasion she had walked into the Coach and Horses at around midnight. An argument ensued as the two left the pub and he began to beat her as they walked down the street. A passer-by intervened and, having stopped the abuse, took them to a local drinking place known only as 'Smith's House'. But Stanton, incensed at what he saw as his grandmother's interference, grasped her by the hair and beat her to the ground with his fists. The old lady, obviously somewhat bruised by the assault, then followed him into the White Horse, where she suffered a third beating. The fourth, final and most brutal attack took place out in the street. In the dock Stanton told the judge, 'I suppose I'm guilty but I don't know what I didn't do.' The judge, rather pompously, told the jury that it was found in dealing with rough people that they said more than they generally meant, and in this case it would not be safe to convict on what lawyers called 'express malice'. It saved Solomon Stanton's life, though it was clearly an injustice to his grandmother. The jury returned a verdict of 'guilty of manslaughter', and he was sentenced to twenty years' imprisonment.

4 MARCH   **1763**   William Swift, a Doncaster labourer, was whipped in front of a large crowd for the theft of five ducks, which he had stolen from local farmer Samuel Baddiley of Bentley.

5 MARCH   **1847**   An explosion ripped through Oaks Colliery, Barnsley, after gas had been accidentally ignited by a naked flame inside the old workings, some 750ft below ground. Of the ninety-seven miners working in an adjacent shaft, seventy-three were killed instantly. Sixty-five of those killed were under the age of 40.

1858   In a rather peculiar case, Henry Wrigley (aged 28) and Joseph Senior (aged 37) stood before the bench having been accused of highway robbery. But this was not a case of the usual type. The two men had assaulted and robbed George Hall as he walked along the road at Thurgoland. Unprofitably for them he had no money, only a 2ft rule, which they stole. Had they discarded it later, they would probably never have been brought to justice, but six months after the robbery Henry Wrigley met a stonemason, a man with a need for a 2ft rule. Having kept the stolen rule at his home, Wrigley promptly retrieved it from its hiding place and sold it for a profit. The stonemason, by the name of Patterson, was seen using it by local police and, as they say, the rest is history. Because no proof could be offered against Joseph Senior, he was released, but his partner in crime went to prison for six months.

Old Yorkshire Beliefs, Omens and Sayings

Never put on a new coat or suit without first placing some pennies in the right-hand pocket. This ensures that the pocket will always be full; but if the pennies are placed in the left-hand pocket, the wearer will never have money so long as the garment is worn.

Old police box at Crosspool. (*Sheffield Libraries, Archives and Local Studies*)

8 MARCH **1782** Frank Fearn was executed on this day for the murder of watchmaker Nathan Andrews in Sheffield. As a warning to others who may have been tempted to transgress, his body was then placed inside an iron cage and hung from a gibbet at Hoxley Edge.

9 MARCH **1902** An inquest was held in Doncaster into the tragic death of Jane Phillipson. Husband Thomas was an accomplished boatman who plied his trade between the port of Hull and Doncaster town, using the Navigation Canal. Often he took along his wife and daughter Minnie. Twenty-four hours earlier they had moored the barge near Doncaster's marketplace at a little after 5.30 p.m., so that Jane could walk into town to buy groceries and provisions. Over the next four hours her husband busied himself with jobs on the boat. Minnie fell asleep and neither seemed to notice that the weekly shopping had taken far longer than had ever been the norm. In fact it was not until 9.30 p.m. that they both realised she had not returned. Trimming a lamp, Thomas Phillipson, suddenly dreading the worst, fetched men from a nearby warehouse and they began a search of the quayside. Within minutes they had found the shopping basket, still packed with the day's purchases, bobbing up and down in the water. Half an hour later one of the men pulled Jane's body from the canal. It appeared she had slipped while climbing down the ladder from the canal side to the deck and had become wedged between boat and bank.

10 MARCH **1858** Joseph Wrightson (27), Thomas Beachill (42), John Foster (30), Edward Wild (24), Thomas Johnson and Joseph Hebden appeared at the Assize Court charged with burgling Flash House Farm at Cawthorne, and in the process attempting to murder the farmer, Joseph Clarkson. The seventh member of the gang, John Hilton, a man well known to police, had been arrested at his home in Barnsley within hours of the robbery being discovered. It was his testimony, once he had decided to become an approver (turn Queen's evidence), which had put them all in the dock. Hilton knew full well the severity of the sentence if he were found guilty alongside the accused, and had never stopped talking from the moment he had been arrested. None of the proceeds from the robbery had been recovered but all the masks used for disguise and the bloodstained clothing worn by the attackers had been found, hidden in a drainage ditch, after Hilton had taken officers to a field on the Dodworth road. It took the jury only a few minutes to declare the six guilty, and all were sentenced to death. The sentence was later commuted to life imprisonment.

11 MARCH **1838** Joseph Greaves, Joseph Brown and Henry Coldwell stood before Sheffield magistrates charged with robbery. They had all been caught shortly after breaking into Joshua Hoyles's cloth store in Yellow Lion Yard, Haymarket, and stealing a large amount of cloth, which they believed they would be able to sell on at a profit. Ill-advisedly they had chosen bonfire night to carry out the burglary, believing that most of Sheffield would be otherwise occupied. In the event, they were very wrong, as they were caught with the stolen goods on the same night. Magistrates referred the case to the Assize Court where the gang was later sentenced to fifteen years' transportation to Australia.

1864 This day brought tragic loss of life in a flood in Sheffield. The 100ft-high dam on Dale Dyke Reservoir, 1 mile in length and containing over 114 million gallons of water, burst just after midnight. The enormous volume of water thundered down the valley, sweeping away houses, mills and businesses. By dawn on this day much of the Don valley was under water and 250 people had drowned, most being caught still asleep in their beds. Rotherham suffered heavy flooding, with Bridgegate completely submerged; it was here that many of Sheffield's dead were found when the waters finally receded. The total economic cost to the city was in excess of £500,000.

12 MARCH

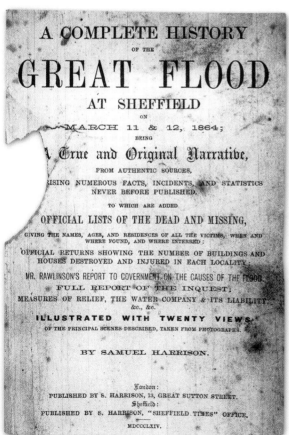

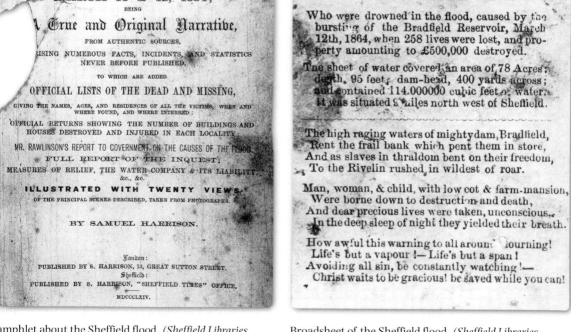

Pamphlet about the Sheffield flood. (*Sheffield Libraries, Archives and Local Studies*)

Broadsheet of the Sheffield flood. (*Sheffield Libraries, Archives and Local Studies*)

13 MARCH **1858** Sheffield man Charles Wright (aged 20) had taken offence when 15-year-old Mary Wright (no relation) called him names in the street. Chasing after her, he knocked her to the ground and kicked her sharply in the side before shouting at her to leave him alone. For Charles that was the end of the matter; retribution had been swift and effective. Leaving the young girl lying in the street, he went about his business and returned home. But the retribution was as deadly as it was swift: the kick to her side had caused considerable internal bleeding and, despite the intervention of a local doctor, Mary died hours later. Charles was subsequently arrested and charged with her manslaughter. At the Assize Court before Mr Justice Byles, he was found guilty and sentenced to one calendar month's imprisonment with hard labour. There were mitigating circumstances, according to the judge: not only had it been in an unguarded moment that Charles Wright had deprived Mary of her life, but also he was still only a young man.

14 MARCH **1837** The trial of Joseph Farmer, a butcher who ran a shop in Fargate, Sheffield, ended with a guilty verdict. But the jury decided that when, in a fit of temper, he had stabbed to death his stepson, Joseph Wilkes, he had not been responsible for his actions and therefore must have been insane. The judge sentenced him to be detained at His Majesty's pleasure and he was sent to St Luke's Asylum, London.

15 MARCH **1837** It was agreed on this day and recorded in the Watch Committee minutes that the duties of Doncaster's gaoler, who had died in February, were to be taken over by his wife. She was to receive one guinea a week for the work, and her role was to be reappraised in April.

16 MARCH **1839** John and William Liversedge of Rawmarsh, Rotherham, were found guilty of burglary at a house in Thrybergh. Persistent offenders and known housebreakers, they were sentenced to be transported to the Australian penal colonies for life.

17 MARCH **Old Yorkshire Cures**
A lump of fresh quicklime the size of a walnut is dropped into a pint of water and allowed to stand all night. The water, having been poured off from the sediment and mixed with a quarter pint of best vinegar, is applied to the head and rubbed into the hair roots and will cure any kind of scurf to the head.

18 MARCH **1871** Reported on this day was the brutal murder of Thomas Lomas by long-term mental patient, George Lawton. Eight years of incarceration had done nothing to improve the mental health of the murderer who, in a fit of uncontrolled anger, snatched a poker from the fireside and beat Thomas Lomas to death during an unprovoked attack. The court recognised his state of mind and declared him insane.

1841 Due to be executed for the murder of Barnsley farmer George Blackburn   19 MARCH
at his farm at Bank Top, John Mitchell, who had denied his guilt throughout
his trial, made a full confession. At the last minute the death sentence was
commuted to transportation for life.

1887 Isaac Hazlehurst was found guilty of the manslaughter of his wife Mary   20 MARCH
Ann, after beating her to death, reported the *Rotherham Advertiser*. He was sent
to prison for eighteen months.

1840 It was agreed by Doncaster's Watch Committee that night watchman   21 MARCH
Walter Wheater be awarded £1 for an act of bravery, after he had been stabbed
while carrying out an arrest.

1919 Constable Paxton, summoned to meet Inspector Bellamy on Mex-   22 MARCH
borough's high street, was told that they were to arrest John Bond (aged 22),
a railwayman both of them knew well. Bond was known to be violent – he had
deserted from the army twice in 1918 and was handy with his fists – but when
the two policemen knocked on his door they had not thought that he would be
armed. As soon as Bond saw the uniform, he pulled a revolver from his pocket,
pressed it against PC Paxton's chest and pulled the trigger. There was a heart-
stopping moment, then a click – the gun had failed to fire. Inspector Bellamy
instantly struck out, knocking Bond to the floor. The police officers managed
to get handcuffs on him and march him back to the police station. When police
later examined the revolver, they found that it was fully loaded. But the bullet in
the firing chamber was observed to be bent, which was why it had misfired – and
saved the life of the constable.

1906 The trial of Harold (Harry) Walters (aged 39) opened before Mr Justice   23 MARCH
Walton. Walters was in the dock for the brutal murder of his lover, Sarah Ann
McConnell, who had been found dead on the hearthrug in the furnished room
she rented at Allen Street, Sheffield. She had been savagely attacked and raped.
Walters denied the murder, insisting he had found her dead at 5.30 p.m. when
he had returned from the pub. But 11-year-old Margaret Osborne, who had
been sent to the house by her mother earlier in the day to collect an outstanding
debt, had seen him kneeling beside the body. Local fish hawker Margaret Revill
told the court she had heard Walters threaten to kill Sarah on the day she had
been murdered. Subsequent forensic examinations also revealed extensive blood
staining on his clothing. The jury returned a verdict of guilty, and the sentence
passed upon Walters was death.

1852 Annie Smith and her 10-month-old baby were found dead at their home   24 MARCH
in Barnsley. According to reports, it was believed that she had murdered her
child and committed suicide while temporarily insane.

1890 Appalling cruelty to children at a Kimberworth house was revealed in   25 MARCH
court. Magistrates heard how John and Elizabeth Bamforth had all but killed

Kimberworth village, home to John and Elizabeth Bamforth, 1900. *(Rotherham Archives and Local Studies)*

five of their seven children through neglect. Sergeant Brooks of Kimberworth police told the court that there had been only a table and two chairs in a downstairs room; nothing else was to be found in the whole house. The entire family was forced to sleep on a stone floor in the kitchen without any means of cover, and the children had no shoes, socks or underwear. Yet the father had been in regular employment and earned sufficient to provide what was needed in the home. According to the police doctor, the house was in a disgusting condition and absolutely filthy throughout, with human excrement lying on the kitchen floor. Magistrates sentenced the parents to three months' imprisonment.

26 MARCH **1859** John Waller, a collier of Thorpe Hesley, was found guilty of being in possession of a pheasant without holding a licence to deal in game. According to the Game Law Act pheasants could not be killed after 1 February, and it was unlawful for any person not licensed to have in his possession any game bird more than forty days after it ought to have been lawfully killed. Waller claimed he had not killed the bird, but had bought it for half a crown from a man in the village; however, he refused to say who that man was. The magistrate pointed out that it was also an offence to buy a pheasant from any other unlicensed person, and fined Waller 20s.

1880 John Gillott, London journalist, district boxer, all-round athlete and son of Rotherham's highly respected police superintendent, was murdered in the Tontine Hotel, Sheffield.

27 MARCH

South Yorkshire Spell to Cast Out Witches

28 MARCH

If troubled by a witch, recite the following:

> Fire dim, fire gan.
> Curling smeak keep o't'pan;
> Here's a teead, there's a frog,
> An' t'eart frev a crimson ask:
> Here's a teeath fra t'heead,
> O' yan 'at's deead,
> 'At nivver gat thruff his task;
> Here's pricked i' blood a maiden's prayer,
> At t'e'e O'man maunt see;
> It's pricked reet thruff a yet warm mask
> Lapt aboot a breet green ask,
> An' it's all foor him an' thee,
> It boils, thoo'll drink,
> He'll speak, thoo'll think,
> It boils, thoo'll see,
> He'll speak, thoo'll dee.
> (Ask – nowt)

1787 John Kenyon was executed at York for burglary. In considering the long record of crime that was already behind him, the court took the view that no amount of time spent in prison would change his ways. The judge therefore passed the sentence of death and told him to prepare himself for his final journey. As a thief he had proved incompetent: after breaking into John Stock's shop in Barnsley two weeks earlier, he had been so noisy that he had been caught in the act.

29 MARCH

1865 William Wilson (a grinder aged 21), Uriah Nelson (a bricklayer aged 27) and Joseph Beardshall (aged 23) all stood in the dock accused of night poaching. They had been caught in Wharncliffe Woods by a group of gamekeepers who had lain in wait. It was an open-and-shut case. All three had been armed: one with a shotgun, one with a hedge-slasher and the third with a pocketful of stones. Mr Justice Willes, however, seemed more concerned with the manner of their arrest and, after sentencing the poachers to three months' imprisonment, verbally attacked the gamekeepers over the use of violence to effect the capture. He told them all in no uncertain terms that had a charge of assault been levelled at them, he would have had no hesitation in sending them to prison too. No doubt suitably chastised, the gamekeepers left court with the judge's condemnation ringing in their ears, though it is unlikely to have had any long-term effects on their future actions.

30 MARCH

31 MARCH **1859** The people of Sheffield read of a case of murder in their city. George Plant, a brewer's traveller, had already been found guilty by a Sheffield coroner's court of the wilful murder of William Wilson. Plant had met Wilson, a brass-caster by trade, while out drinking in the city, and after a heated argument the two men fought with each other at the bottom of Hartshead. Fearing for his life, Plant claimed he had been forced to use a knife that he always carried in case of attack, but had not intended to kill; the coroner's jury had disagreed. However, at his trial the presiding judge took the view that, while it may have been reasonable to conclude that Plant had stabbed the unfortunate brass-worker to death, there was insufficient evidence to show that it had been a deliberate act. Accordingly, having instructed the jury to return a manslaughter verdict, he passed a sentence on Plant of transportation for life.

APRIL

The funeral of the Kimberworth murder victims, 20 November 1912 (see 23 April).
(Rotherham Archives and Local Studies)

1 APRIL **1868** Eleven people, including six children, were killed on this day at the fireworks factory, Doncaster Road, Barnsley, after gunpowder kept in a tin was accidentally placed on the top of a hot stove. The factory consisted of three sheds: one of these had been full of children aged between 9 and 16, employed in filling up firework cases; the other two had been used as store rooms for empty firework cases. All were totally destroyed. Similarly flattened was a detached stone house known locally as the magazine, because of the amount of gunpowder and brimstone stored in its rooms.

2 APRIL **1899** A horrific murder was committed at Cliffe Quarry, Monk Bretton, on this day. The dead body of Ann Whitehead (aged 63) was discovered some few hours after her death. Police believed her killer to be one Tom Wormald, a man she knew, and he was subsequently arrested. But at his trial, the jury found Wormald innocent and the case was dismissed. In a tragic postscript, however, Wormald drowned himself in January 1900.

3 APRIL **1894** James Billington, Britain's executioner, placed the noose around the neck of Philip Garner at 8 a.m. and pulled the lever that released the trapdoor beneath his feet, executing the Doncaster killer. Garner had been found guilty of the murder of his wife, Agnes, after they had both returned from a night's drinking in the Lord Nelson public house at Norton. It had been a troubled marriage from the outset: the two had split up on numerous occasions but had lately decided to stay together. For Agnes, it was to prove a tragic decision. After walking her to a quiet area, known locally as Low Pastures, Garner had beaten her to death with a hammer.

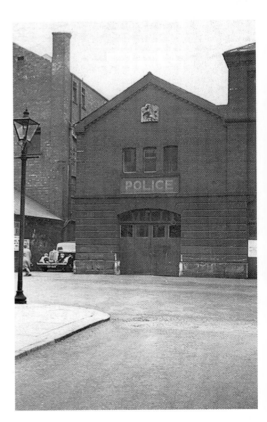

4 APRIL **1893** Edward Hemmings (aged 26) was executed for the murder of his wife Annie in their rented room at Woodhouse. Jealous of the attentions she had paid to the other three lodgers in the house, he hit her over the head with an axe, slit her throat, then left her dead in front of the fireplace. Though Hemmings had never denied his guilt, the jury nevertheless recommended mercy. The plea fell on deaf ears.

Doncaster police lock-up, 1920. (Reproduced by kind permission of Doncaster Library and Information Services)

HORRIBLE WIFE MURDER
BY A
TREETON COLLIER.

A JEALOUS HUSBAND.

FLIGHT AND CAPTURE OF THE MURDERER.

LATEST DETAILS.

[By Our Own Reporters]

Great consternation was caused throughout the neighbourhood of Woodhouse, on Thursday, by the horrible murder of a young woman named Annie Hemmings. The perpetrator of the shocking deed was the poor creature's husband, who is, by trade a collier, and who, for some time, has been employed at the Treeton Pit of the Rother Vale Collieries Company, The victim, a bride of only eight months, met her death on the anniversary of the day of her birth. She was twenty-one years of age on Thursday. The couple had lodged at the house of Mr. and Mrs. Charles Everidge Kennington, in Furnace lane, Woodhouse. Kennington, who is in the employment of the M. S. and L. Railway Company, at Beighton Station, has several lodgers. Edward Hemmings and his wife had a room on the ground floor which was used both as a sitting room and bed room, and in which were their own belongings. In this place the Hemmings had been living for the last five weeks. The husband was some four years older than his wife. Their married life began in June last, but this had been interrupted by various separations, and one or two little households had been broken up. Part of the time had been spent in lodgings at the house of the young woman's married sister at Woodhouse Mill, only a short distance away. It would appear that had Hemmings been a man of another stamp a comfortable little home might have been in the possession of the young couple, and the more immediate supposed cause of this shocking event would thus have been absent. In the same house were, as has been stated, other lodgers. These were single young men. Now, so far as can be gathered, there is no ground whatever for believing that the young wife had in any way been guilty of conduct that might be expected to arouse a deadly jealousy on her husband's part. But she was a woman of cheerful pleasant disposition, fond of company and conversation, and of her own solitariness, she frequently passed into another room, where she engaged in conversation with her landlady and with the other lodgers. The husband was a silent, morose man, self-contained in disposition, seldom holding much conversation with his wife or his fellows, and it would seem he was annoyed at his wife leaving their own room in this manner to enjoy the company of others. He had, in fact, said as much to his wife's sister. Whether any serious disturbance had arisen between the pair on this account or not is hardly yet clear. The husband was not a demonstrative man, while she was a hearty ...

Billington, the executioner, allowed him a 7ft 5in drop because of his weight: though slimmer than at his trial when he weighed in at over 11 stone.

1861 After a robbery that went terribly wrong, Samuel Mitchell was convicted and sentenced to death for the brutal murder of 78-year-old Ralph Barber in a Sheffield street.

5 APRIL

1837 At a meeting of the Doncaster Watch Committee it was agreed that all police sergeants and constables be paid an additional 5s for the apprehension of every person charged with felony brought before a magistrate and committed for trial or held on bail. A further 2s 6d was also to be paid for every mile travelled from their station in order to serve a warrant or summons.

6 APRIL

1865 It was reported in the *Doncaster Chronicle* that Thomas Topham and his wife Sarah appeared before magistrates, charged with obtaining money under false pretences. Thomas was the local secretary in Rotherham of the Amalgamated Society of Engineers. Travelling members were entitled to donations on arrival in certain towns on presenting their membership cards to the secretary, who then gave them a cheque drawn upon the local treasury. Sarah induced a woman to present three forged cheques to Thomas, each worth 4s 2d and all signed using false names. He in turn paid out and recorded the transactions. Although the police were sure of Thomas's guilt, the magistrates disagreed. A closer examination of the records showed that Thomas had not been in Rotherham when his wife's co-conspirator presented the cheques. He was set free – but Sarah went to prison for nine months.

7 APRIL

Headline describing Annie Hemmings' murder. (*Barnsley Chronicle*)

8 APRIL, **1786** Robert Watson (aged 22) was executed for the highway robbery of William Bailes on the Rotherham to Barnsley road. After knocking the man down, he beat him with a club, threatened his life and stole 7½ guineas from his person.

9 APRIL, **1838** During a fierce thunderstorm over Barnsley Cross Pit, Silkstone was flooded and twenty-six unfortunate miners were swept to their deaths below ground.

10 APRIL, **1835** An inquest held at the Falstaff Inn, Wicker, into the death of William Simonite, beerhouse keeper of Willey Street, concluded that he had been murdered by John Unwin. Three days earlier, Unwin, who lived a street away, walked into the beerhouse and asked for a gallon of ale. He was refused on the grounds that it was late in the week. He left but returned some hours later showing obvious signs of intoxication and demanded a pint of beer. Rebecca Simonite told the coroner that when her husband, William, refused to serve him a second time because of the state he was in, there was a brief scuffle resulting in Unwin being physically ejected. After shouting verbal abuse from outside, he again walked into the beerhouse and again the two fought; but this time Unwin struck William Simonite a fatal blow to the stomach. Surgeon Mr Wright Wilson told the court that the blow had ruptured a number of

Wheatley Lane, Doncaster, c. 1900. (Reproduced by kind permission of Doncaster Library and Information Services)

vital organs just below the heart, and death had been inevitable, but that the attacker would not have realised the extent to which he had injured the unfortunate landlord. The coroner agreed and returned a verdict of manslaughter.

1858 The *Rotherham and Masbrough Advertiser* reported the inquest into the suicide of cutlery manufacturer Edward Hobson of Snighill. According to the coroner's report, Hobson had walked the streets during Sunday morning chatting to various neighbours whose doors were open because of the warm weather, until he came across Simon Godfrey's shop. Here he asked the young owner if he would lend him a razor, explaining that because it was Sunday he felt awkward about visiting a barber's shop. Godfrey was at first reluctant – Edward Hobson was a stranger to him – but after a little persuasive argument and a shilling left on his counter as a token deposit, he agreed. Promising to return, Hobson then took the razor, walked to a passageway across the street and promptly slit his throat.

11 APRIL

Scotland Street gaol bread warrant. (*Sheffield Libraries, Archives and Local Studies*)

The following QUERIES must be satisfactorily answered by the Prisoner making Application for **BREAD**.

Scotland-Street Gaol,

183

QUERIES.	ANSWERS.
1. What is your Name and Trade?	1. *Thos Priest*
2. Who sent you to Gaol?	2. *Mr Johnson*
3. Are you sued in the High or Low Court?	3. *Low Court*
4. What is the Term of Imprisonment?	4. *60 Days*
5. Will you apply to be discharged under the Insolvent Act?	5. *no*
6. Have you any Property?	6. *no*
7. Are you a Pensioner?	7. *no*
8. Who was your last Employer?	8. *Geo Priest*
9. Are you working in Gaol?	9. *no*
10. Have you any Apprentices?	10. *no*
11. Where does your Family reside?	11. *Sheffield*
12. State the Number and Ages of your Children?	12. *One Child about 10 months*
13. State the Place of Settlement, and how acquired?	13. *By Servitude*

He was not bound apprentice and his father belongs Sheffield

12 APRIL   **1836**   *Killed for a penny pie.* John Ducker (aged 20) stood in the dock accused of murdering John Rathmel in the White Swan Inn, Doncaster, after buying a one-penny pie from him. He claimed the pie seller had refused to give him the 2d change to which he was entitled, despite his protestations at the injustice of being short-changed. The two argued, and then, in a fit of temper, John Ducker struck several blows, most hitting the pieman on the head. It was one of these blows, according to medical evidence, that had killed him. Ducker was lucky: the judge, after hearing all the evidence, decided that though he had been responsible for the death, he had not intended it. Manslaughter was the jury's verdict, and a sentence of six months was handed down.

13 APRIL   **1737**   At Doncaster Courthouse, John Maxfield was found guilty of stealing one silver spoon and one linen napkin, valued at 2s, from neighbour John Gill. Justice was swift and extremely painful. The magistrates ordered he be taken to the marketplace and whipped.

14 APRIL   **1839**   Reported on this day by the *Sheffield Mercury* was the death of John Blackwell in Sheffield's poorhouse, where he had lived for his final eight years. Famous throughout his youth as Jackey Blackey the 'King of the Gallery', the man who had dominated the Sheffield stage, he had latterly fallen on hard times. A central figure during the bread riots of 1816, when he had joined crowds demonstrating against the price of bread, he had been arrested by Lord Wharncliffe for daring to carry a blood-smeared loaf of bread on a pole high above the heads of the crowd. The act brought two years' imprisonment for incitement and caused his inevitable downfall. Back in prison four years later for inciting yet more rioting, but this time while armed, Blackwell was forced into penury and died a poor man.

15 APRIL   **1880**   Joseph Moulson, farmer, was fined 2s 6d at Doncaster police court for riding without reins along the Adwick Road and warned of the consequences of furious driving.

16 APRIL   **1837**   Unusual deaths in Sheffield were reported on this day. Grinder William Wilkinson died of hydrophobia (rabies) after being attacked and bitten by his own dog. Worse still, passer-by James Ibbotson, who had tried to stop the attack, died on the same day from bites he had received in the rescue attempt. The double deaths spelled bad news for Sheffield's dogs: any found loose from that time on were rounded up and destroyed.

17 APRIL   **1897**   Louisa Williams murdered George South (aged 47) by beating him to death with a rolling pin after a row about his drinking habits. At her trial it was accepted that she had not intended to kill the man and a charge of manslaughter was accepted by the judge. She was sent to prison for an unreported period of time.

1605   Joan Jurdie (aged 52) received scant reward for the help she had given her neighbours over the years. Brought before Major Hughe Childers at Doncaster, she was accused by them of practising witchcraft and being responsible for the deaths of Jenett Murfin and her newly born child. Called to the house by Jenett's husband Peter because his wife had endured a difficult and painful birth, Joan had waited three days before making the visit, during which time mother and child had grown ever more ill. Then, when she did at last arrive, all she did was lie beside the critically ill woman and her baby for a short time before leaving again. The woman's breast milk turned to blood and she refused all food, claiming 'I was ridden by with a witch, and therefore I could never eate any meate' and died shortly afterwards. Just for good measure the neighbours also threw in the double deaths of a mother and daughter from the previous year, Hester and Jane Dolphin, whom they claimed Joan had cursed. Happily for her, though, Major Childers was unconvinced by all the claims and took the view than none of it could be proved. Joan was therefore released back into the bosom of her so-called friends.

1890   A report appeared in the *Rotherham Advertiser* of the court appearance of William Pritchard and his wife Mary Ann who had been brought to court accused of atrocious cruelty to children. William, their youngest son (aged 1), had been carried into a doctor's surgery suffering from scarlet fever. According to the doctor who saw the child, he gave instructions on how to cure the condition and provided a list of medicines the family was to obtain. Five days later he visited the house, which he described as a filthy hole, and found the little boy dead. He told Mary Ann, who had made no attempt to buy the necessary medicines, that she had neglected her son and caused his death. Despite this, he signed the death certificate. When, five days later, the youngest daughter, Jemima, died of exactly the same condition and again after ignoring his advice, the doctor called in the police. Magistrates, after listening to the doctor tell the court that in his opinion the children might as well have been murdered, imposed a sentence of two months' hard labour.

1856   John Smith and Henry Holmes Vaughan, fork-grinders, stood before magistrates in Sheffield charged with rattening, a serious offence of smashing new machinery, committed because both men had objected vigorously to the introduction of more automation at their place of work. They had attempted to destroy as many of the new machines as possible because they believed that automation would eventually put them out of work. Each received a prison sentence of one year for their actions.

1841   An inquest opened at the Canal Tavern, Mexborough, into the murder of widow Ann Scoran (aged 62). Discovered dying in her own home, she had been attacked as she opened her front door to what she thought were her lodgers. Witnesses told the court that there had been a commotion in the street after two men had begun throwing stones at the window of the house, then knocking loudly at the door. Once the old lady had realised that her callers were not her lodgers, she had apparently returned indoors to fetch a gun, which she intended to use to scare the men off. However, this proved ineffectual, for, once the two had seen the firearm, they hurled stones at her, attacked her on the doorstep, bundled her into the house and, after forcing the gun from her grasp, beat her to death with it. The two men, William Hepworth and George Eastwood, both aged 20, were brought to the court and publicly identified by a number of local people who claimed to have seen them in the street, despite the dark night. But the most damning piece of evidence was presented by the lodger who rented an upper room and who had eventually found Ann lying in a pool of blood just inside her own doorway. He told the jury that with her dying breath she had named the two men responsible for the attack, and that the names she had given were those of the accused. A coroner's warrant for wilful murder was issued. At their eventual trial the men pleaded mitigating circumstances. They had, they claimed, been forced to defend themselves against her because they believed they were going to be shot. The defence was accepted and a verdict of manslaughter returned by the jury. The judge took a lenient view and sent the killers to prison for two months.

22 APRIL   **1841**   Readers of the *Sheffield and Rotherham Independent* learned of the death of William Hubbard, believed by many to have murdered his cousin and lover, Eliza Grimwood. Years earlier, the paper had published several articles regarding the police investigation into her killing and the several attempts to bring him to justice. Each arrest had failed because of a lack of evidence. Despite the police belief that he had been the murderer, there had never been any corroborative evidence to substantiate the charge. On his deathbed he had apparently cried out to Eliza, claiming he could see her in his bedroom. Whether or not this story was true, Hubbard never went so far as to confess to the murder.

23 APRIL   **1913**   Walter Sykes was executed on this day for the murder of two children, Amy Collinson (aged 10) and Frances Nicholson (aged 7). Both girls had been found dead, their throats cut, after attending a carol concert rehearsal at Kimberworth. Cousins, the girls lived only a mile apart, Frances in a terraced cottage beneath the Keppel's Column monument, known locally as Scholes Coppice, and Amy at Abdy Farm on Kimberworth Park Road. Firm friends, they rarely went anywhere unless they were in each other's company. The concert had been arranged by their school at Meadowhall and the girls, despite the reservations of their parents, were desperate to be allowed to attend. Aware of their excitement, the two sets of parents had eventually agreed. Isaac Nicholson, Frances's father, told the Collinsons that he would send her brothers over to the farm at around 8 p.m. to collect her and then walk with her back to the house at Scholes. All the two girls then had to do was walk back to the farmhouse from Kimberworth Church after the concert, a distance of no more than a mile and a half. When they had not arrived by the agreed time, the two Nicholson boys were sent out to find them. When they returned empty-handed,

Opposite, top: The Colin Campbell pub at Kimberworth, near where the little girls were last seen, 1912.

Opposite, bottom: Keppel's Column at Scholes.

Abdy Farm where Amy Collinson lived, 1912. (R. Newton)

a search was launched that grew in size and went on throughout the night. The bodies of the two little girls were finally discovered beneath a hedgerow by the two mothers at dawn the following morning, some hundred yards from the back door of the farm.

At the inquest the court was told that the elder of the two had been raped some two or three days earlier. This gave police a probable motive for the double murder. The profile of the killer they then produced was of a man who knew the children, possibly well, someone they trusted and a man whose motive could well have been simply to silence them. After six weeks of fruitless investigation by the police, Walter Sykes had walked into a police station and confessed his guilt. Strangely though, and what would later make the case so unusual and notorious, Sykes, a man of low intellect, fitted none of the criteria set by the investigation team. But he did confess – a statement that he subsequently retracted prior to the case being brought before a judge. The evidence, apart from his confession, was purely circumstantial; nothing ever really linked him to the murders. All his clothing was recovered and no blood staining was found; and the knife he claimed to have used to commit the murder was eventually discovered in the possession of a man living in a Rotherham lodging house, to whom Sykes had sold it for 2d. It yielded no clues either. Local people raised a petition after his conviction to have the sentence commuted to life – such was the belief among those in the area that Sykes was not the killer. It made no difference to the verdict and clemency was rejected. Whether his confession was true or false, he died under the watchful eye of executioner Thomas Pierrepoint.

1890 It had been a normal day in the Skinn household. George Skinn had recovered from the influenza that had kept him away from his job as a woodsman at Maltby and now in good spirits he, his daughter Ellen and granddaughter Agnes had enjoyed a convivial evening in front of the fire. When all three retired to bed at about 10 p.m. there was nothing to suggest that everyone would not sit around the same breakfast table on the following morning. But all was far from well, certainly as far as George was concerned. At about 5 a.m. Ellen, who shared her bedroom with her daughter, awoke to see her father enter the room rather furtively with his hands behind his back. As he reached the bed in which the two women slept, he suddenly produced a hammer, raised it above his head and began to beat Agnes about the head. Ellen immediately leapt at him, fought him into a corner of the room and wrestled the hammer from his grasp. Pushing her away, he then ran from the house, out into the garden and threw himself head first into the well. Agnes was extremely fortunate: none of the hammer blows had been life-threatening and eventually she made a full recovery. George on the other hand drowned; his battered body was found later at the bottom of what was described by the *Rotherham Advertiser* as 'a moderately deep well'.

1836 *Uproar in court!* George Cutts was unbelievably found not guilty of the murder of his live-in lover, Mary Ann Gillott, at their Sheffield home. This was despite evidence that in September 1835 he had physically attacked her after she had refused to admit him to the house, striking her with his fists, dragging her back into the house by the hair after she ran away, and finally beating her with a bedpost. Because, in the opinion of the examining surgeon, she had died as a result of a ruptured artery caused by an ulcerated lung, the jury decided that death had been due to natural causes.

1890 An inquest held at the Little Bridge Inn, Parkgate, heard details of the double death by drowning of Agnes Ruston (aged 22) and her 8-month-old baby. Agnes, the jury was told, had left home a year earlier and set up house with a man named John Hooly. She was pregnant with his child at the time and, unfortunately for her, Hooly had little regard for either her or the child she carried. After a disastrous year during which he had beaten her, sold all the furniture, moved her into lodgings, then abandoned her and the newborn infant, she found herself forced into Rotherham workhouse. Desperate for help, she asked her parents to take her in. They refused, insisting she must accept the charity set by the Guardians who administered poor relief. Snatching the baby in a fit of anger, she ran to the canal and drowned it. Her body was recovered from the same canal several days later.

1835 In a published letter to the *Sheffield Independent*, a warden of Sheffield's prison stated that ninety inmates were forced to exercise in a yard measuring 57ft by 24ft. The same number of men had only twenty-four bedsteads and were forced to spend long hours in a single cell that allowed almost no room for movement: in order to straighten their backs they must find a place on the floor

The door to Eccleshall Gaol, near Sheffield. *(Sheffield Libraries, Archives and Local Studies)*

against the cold walls. The average sentence for debts of only a few shillings was three weeks, and if the debt was so much as a penny over £1, they had an extra twenty days added to their sentence.

28 APRIL **Old Yorkshire Beliefs, Omens and Sayings**
A knife must never be given as a present. Unlucky to give, unlucky to receive, it will sever either friendship or love.

29 APRIL **1887** The body of Edward Copley was discovered on this day, after he had been shot by David Copley at Cudworth. It was a year before police were able to find Copley, finally trapping him in Reading. He was sentenced to death for the murder, but the sentence was commuted to life and he was released to freedom in Barnsley in 1898.

30 APRIL **1834** A sentence of death was passed against Thomas Rodgers (aged 26) for having committed an unnatural act with Charles Bennett, the evidence for which, reported the *Sheffield Independent*, was unfit for publication. In pronouncing the sentence, his lordship the judge stated that he had been convicted of 'a crime against which human nature shudders, and at the contemplation of which the mind shrinks back in horror'.

MAY

Police staff, Frederick Street, Rotherham, 1907.
(Rotherham Archives and Local Studies)

1 MAY   **1865**   An inquest opened into the death of a baby boy whose strangled body was found in the toilet of the Three Legs of Man public house. The attending surgeon, Mr Fairbanks, told the Doncaster court that the child was a newborn but had certainly lived. Full-grown, the baby's body measured 16in in length, but marks around the neck showed that either delivery had been unusual or that the child had been murdered by some sort of ligature, which had been used to strangle it. He also told the coroner that he thought it most unlikely that the young woman from Branton currently under suspicion was in fact the birth mother and hence probable killer: medical examination had revealed that she had never given birth to a child. A verdict of unlawful killing was returned.

2 MAY   **1940**   Stephen Wade of Doncaster was appointed assistant executioner, to work alongside Albert and Thomas Pierrepoint.

3 MAY   **1862**   An inquest opened into the murder of 4-year-old William Lincoln, who had been beaten to death by his stepmother, Mary. During the seven weeks since her marriage to William's father and her arrival at the family home, she had managed to break both his thighbones and beat him across most of his body, resulting in his almost inevitable death. She was sentenced to three years' penal servitude.

4 MAY   **1858**   George Hallott of Rawmarsh stood before Rotherham magistrates, accused of robbing Walter Froggart of his most prized possession: his wife. The woman in question, Mary, had been carrying on an affair with the defendant, but had returned to her husband's hearth after claiming that the relationship was over. However, two weeks later the unsuspecting husband was robbed of every stick of furniture he owned. Later that same day, not surprisingly suspecting that she had returned to her lover, he found both of them at Rotherham railway station attempting to move their ill-gotten gains to George Hallott's house. Police were called and Mary and George were arrested. It was argued in court that the household goods had been given by Walter Froggart to his wife six months earlier and she only returned them when she went back to the marital home. To say the wife had done no more than return for her own belongings, ran the argument, was unjust. Therefore the husband could only claim the man she had run to was guilty of the theft of his wife, as she was seen as her husband's chattel. Magistrates decided to release her into her husband's care and they committed Hallott for trial at the Assizes. He was eventually sent to prison for six months.

5 MAY   **1833**   Charles Jackson stood in the dock, accused of the manslaughter of Edward Bower during a prize fight held at Shire Green. Alongside him were Henry Jackson, Joseph Lambert, James Mappin (alias James Muscroft) and William Hindes, who were all charged with aiding and abetting. These four men had set up the fight for a prize of £5 and had acted as seconds. The court was told that after a ring had been formed in a field behind a Shire Green public

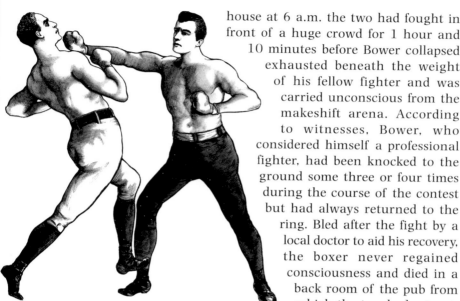

house at 6 a.m. the two had fought in front of a huge crowd for 1 hour and 10 minutes before Bower collapsed exhausted beneath the weight of his fellow fighter and was carried unconscious from the makeshift arena. According to witnesses, Bower, who considered himself a professional fighter, had been knocked to the ground some three or four times during the course of the contest but had always returned to the ring. Bled after the fight by a local doctor to aid his recovery, the boxer never regained consciousness and died in a back room of the pub from which the two had set out. Doctors Jackson and Turton diagnosed death as being caused by a blow to the left side of the temple. The jury returned a verdict of guilty and all the accused were sent to prison in York.

1881 The trial opened on this day, before Mr Justice Kay, of James Hall (aged 53), a Sheffield cutler. Partial to a drink or two, Hall, after an argument with his wife, fetched an axe from the coal shed and struck her several times about the head. She, of course, died as a result. But before he could escape from the house he was disturbed by his stepdaughter returning after a night out with her fiancé. Realising the back door was locked, which she knew to be extremely unusual, she stood in the backyard, knocking until he came to the door with a key. As the door opened and before she had chance to step across the back step, he aimed a misdirected blow at her head, using the same axe. Happily, the blade caught her on the chin but did not knock her to the ground. She needed no second invitation to run, and set off for the street with Hall in close pursuit. Within about 50ft of the house he struck out at her again, this time catching her a telling blow to the centre of her back, which felled her in the middle of the road. Here she was very lucky: Richard Duckenfield, the man she intended to marry, had not had time to walk all the way back to his lodgings and saw the whole event unfold. In one fast and furious charge he managed to tackle her stepfather and pull him away from her prone body before he could deliver the fatal blow. The two men then wrestled on the ground, but James Hall was no match for the younger man, who within minutes had him face down with his arms pinned behind his back, where he stayed until local police arrived. Stepdaughter Selina survived and damned him from the dock. The jury returned a guilty verdict: James Hall was executed two weeks later.

6 MAY

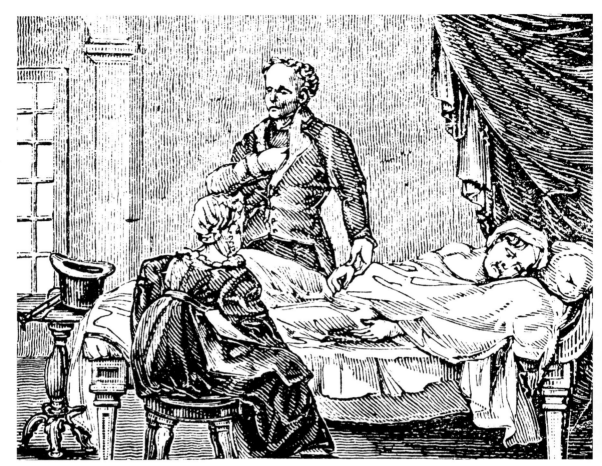

Woodcut of a nineteenth-century physician.

7 MAY **1838** An inquest opened at Park House Farm, Intake, into the murder of Henry Johnson (aged 20), who was killed by a party of rook-stealers during the early hours of the morning. Awoken by the sound of a gunshot, he and most of the farm household left their beds to investigate. In a rookery which lay in a small croft beside the farmhouse, he and the farmer, a Mr Ward, clearly saw a group of men silhouetted against the night sky and began shouting at them to leave. Realising they were being ignored, he, the farmer and a house servant went to the barn and collected a hay fork each. Before the three managed to get into the croft, they were ambushed by the rook-stealers and in the running fight that ensued, the forks were wrested from their hands. Perhaps because Johnson had put up the greatest resistance, the thieves beat him unconscious with one of the forks' long shafts. He was found later by the farmer and carried back to the house. Three Sheffield surgeons were called to the house and all predicted his imminent death from a serious fracture of the skull on the right side of his

head. He lived a further four days without ever regaining full consciousness. Six men were arrested within hours of the murder and the coroner's jury named two men, reported only as Herod and Jones, as guilty of manslaughter, with four others guilty of aiding and abetting. They were to stand trial at the Autumn Assizes.

1831 Robert Yardley and Luke Sadler, convicted of setting fire to a stack of oats at Sheffield, were sentenced to death at their trial in York.

1834 Joseph Senior (aged 30) and John Shaw (aged 39) were found guilty of stealing a brown horse from farmer Joseph Scholey's farm at Edlington, Doncaster. The two men were spotted some 22 miles away from the scene of their crime on the following morning. Recognised as known thieves, they were promptly arrested. The judge passed a sentence of transportation to the Australian colonies for life.

1825 Reported in the *Doncaster Review* was the strange inscription on the headstone of blacksmith George Naffaw of Sprotborough who died this day.

> My sledge hammer lies declined,
> My bellows too, have lost their wind,
> My fire's extinct, my forge decayed,
> My vice now in the dust is laid,
> My iron and my coals are gone,
> My nails are drove, my work done,
> My fire-dried corpse lies here at rest,
> My soul is waiting to be blest.

1858 An inquest heard that 16-year-old Walter Wilson had been found hanging in the rabbit shed at the back of the White Swan public house on Westgate, Rotherham, by the landlady, his aunt Hannah Jackson. Wilson had been adopted along with his sister by the Jacksons after his father, a well-known chimney sweep, had died some years earlier. Unhappy with his life at the pub, he had taken to staying away whenever he could and for the four weeks prior to his death had been somewhat depressed, according to his aunt. Others claimed that the reason for killing himself had little to do with the family and more to do with the company he had been keeping. Sarah Tattersall, a good friend of the family and a woman who had known him since childhood, concurred and described him as 'a rather stupid boy'. The coroner recorded a verdict of suicide.

1641 A son of Yorkshire, Thomas Wentworth, 1st Earl of Strafford, was executed on this day on Tower Hill before a crowd of 200,000 people. A one-time friend of Charles I and forever a royalist, he loathed corruption, craved order and was an advocate of the rule of law. Betrayed by his king and condemned by his parliament, he accepted his fate with incredible bravery. After removing his doublet and winding his hair under a white cap, he thanked

8 MAY

9 MAY

10 MAY

11 MAY

12 MAY

Thomas Wentworth, 1st Earl of Strafford. *(Brian Elliott Collection)*

the executioner for the job he was to do, telling him he would fit his neck to the block before laying his head down to better aid the axe. The crowd fell suddenly silent as the Earl knelt and did as he had said. Then, with one stroke of the executioner's blade, the head fell from his body. Wentworth's remains were carried back to South Yorkshire later that same night and buried secretly.

A monument was later erected in the old church at Wentworth Woodhouse. Perhaps his greatest epitaph came from France, where Cardinal Richelieu said of him, 'The English were so foolish that they killed their wisest man.'

Wentworth Woodhouse, Rotherham. *(By arrangement with Geoffrey Howse & Walker's Newsagents (Hoyland) Collection)*

1859 A court heard a tale of highway robbery at Doncaster. Paul Tearney (aged 25), John Webster (aged 22), Ellen Brewell (aged 17) and Ellen Gregory (aged 19) were found guilty before Mr Justice Hill of robbery and assault against John Oakerfull, robbing him of 11s on the Doncaster road. Tearney received four years' penal servitude while his younger accomplices got three.

13 MAY

1897 The *Mexborough and Swinton Times* reported the murder of Florence Robinson at Monk Bretton, Barnsley. Husband Joseph (aged 30) was arrested by police within hours of the body's discovery. The couple had separated, and the fact that Florence had taken over the role of housekeeper to Joseph's brother had inevitably provided fertile ground for jealousy. Arguments followed and after one particularly nasty exchange, Joseph had walked into Barnsley and bought a revolver. From there, he went straight to his brother's house, marched in and calmly shot his wife dead. Once back at the marital home, he swallowed a large quantity of laudanum – but was found before the drug could do any serious damage. Arrested and brought before magistrates, he was ordered to stand trial at the next Assizes.

14 MAY

1855 Two unidentified men were badly beaten and robbed on the Queen's highway of a significant but undisclosed amount of money, which they were carrying to the Milton and Elsecar Ironworks. The robbers, James Darley and James Ashton, had lain in wait for them at Wentworth Park, having been tipped off about the unusually large amount of coin they were transporting. Inept at their trade, and identified by the victims, both were caught within twenty-four hours and all the money recovered. As the price for their failure as highway robbers, the judge sentenced Ashton, who had a record of street crime, to hard labour for four years, and his confederate to six years.

15 MAY

1880 A fatal accident occurred near Doncaster railway station. Thomas Cole, an employee of the Great Northern Railway, was returning to work after his breakfast and took a short cut across the railway lines instead of using the road. As he approached the Nine Arch Bridge he stepped from one line to another in order to avoid the Manchester to Lincoln train. His mistake was that he had forgotten the newspaper express. Thomas was killed instantly, his body being literally torn to pieces by the speeding train.

16 MAY

1880 An inquest opened at Hatfield into the death of Henry Singleton (aged 23). Poor Henry had been jilted by the love of his life, and after eating lunch at home had walked the short distance to a narrow dyke that ran alongside one of the fields on his father's farm. Removing his jacket, he had jumped into just 1ft of water and succeeded in drowning himself. He left behind two letters: one to his parents and one to the girl who had spurned him. The coroner returned a verdict of suicide while in a state of temporary insanity.

17 MAY

1880 George Sneath, manager of Verity's railway wagon company in Mexborough, was charged with manslaughter after admitting to fighting with

18 MAY

three men. One of the men he knocked down struck the back of his head as he fell, fracturing his skull. Unhappily for both George Sneath and his opponent, the injury proved fatal. The verdict of the jury at Sneath's later trial is not recorded.

19 MAY **1837** *Charged with stealing bones.* At the Mansion House, Doncaster, Irishman Michael Hughes and George Baker from Nantes, France, were charged with stealing bones and selling them at 6d a stone in Frenchgate to a furrier for use as manure. Both men denied the charge but they were nevertheless ordered to leave the town immediately or be imprisoned as vagrants.

20 MAY **1831** Thomas Gregg was brought before the court, charged with stealing a flock of sheep and giving perjured evidence in a previous case against an innocent man. Gregg was well known to the court as a persistent offender, liar and waster. Unhesitatingly, the judge put on the black cap and sentenced the prisoner to death, telling him as he did so that he doubted that anyone present in the courtroom, or hearing of the case at a later date, could ever object to a verdict that would forever rid the world of so serious a reprobate.

21 MAY **1873** Sarah Wright and her unborn baby were accidentally killed as they watched Sangars' Circus parade through the streets of Barnsley. Keen to see the animals in their cages, she had stepped out from the crowds lining the pavements, and into the road. Sadly, as the throng pressed forward she was pushed beneath the wheels of the van that was carrying the circus band.

Earlesmere Avenue, Balby, c. 1900. (Reproduced by kind permission of Doncaster Library and Information Services)

WHEREAS on Thursday the 18th instant, Favier Lambertier, and his wife went away from their Lodgings in Campo-Lane Sheffield, and is suspected to have taken some Articles with them in a felonious manner; he is about 45 years of age, 6 feet, high, lean visaged, wears his hair tied, drest either in dark green or light drab, is a native of France, speaks broken English.——
His wife and two children are supposed to be with him, one about two years and a half old, another a year, both boys. He teaches French and Fencing.

NOTICE IS HEREBY GIVEN

Whoever will apprehend the said Favier and his wife, and secure them in any of his Majesty's Gaols in this Kingdom, shall on notice given to J. Crome printer in Sheffield, receive a reward of Five Guineas.
¶‡* There are several charges of felony against them besides.

Note. One Che ham, a Cutler, and his Wife, in Water-Lane, are supposed to be concerned in the above villainous transaction.

November 19th, 1790.

1888 James William Richardson (aged 23), a brickwork labourer, was executed on this day for the murder of works foreman William Berridge. The two men had argued after Richardson had broken a brush in a machine. Berridge accused him of being careless and sent him home. Filled with a sense of injustice, Richardson returned a few hours later, ostensibly to collect his pay packet – but with a loaded revolver in his pocket. The minute he saw William Berridge he pulled out the gun, aimed, shot the man in the head and then calmly walked away. Berridge survived for a few hours before dying later that evening. Arrested the same day, Richardson had no explanation for the shooting other than that he felt he had been unfairly treated and wanted justice. At his trial before Mr Justice Mathew, he failed to offer any other reasonable defence for his actions. The jury had no difficulty in returning a guilty verdict.

22 MAY

Wanted notice, 1790. (Sheffield Libraries, Archives and Local Studies)

1833 A meeting of the overseers of the several townships making up the parish of Sheffield was held at the Sheffield workhouse. It was agreed by the delegates that a petition should be put forward for the abolition of imprisonment for any debt under £5, and for the extension to Sheffield of the government's proposed local courts bill. In support of their demands,

23 MAY

delegates cited the fact that the gaols of both Sheffield and Eccleshall contained on average about 100 persons, who discharged by their imprisonment debts amounting to £1,520 annually, and that the cost to the parish of Sheffield and neighbourhood of maintaining these prisoners and their families amounted to £1,700. The imbalance of almost £200 supported the argument against imprisonment on the grounds that it was not cost-effective to the city.

24 MAY

Peel Square, Barnsley, *c. 1905. (Brian Elliott Collection)*

1841 John Mitchell was sentenced to death for the brutal murder of Barnsley farmer George Blackburn at his farmhouse at Bank Top. Hours before he was to mount the scaffold, he made a full confession, earning himself a reprieve and a change of sentence to one of transportation to Australia for the remainder of his life.

1841   John Hanson was convicted on this day of being found with a counterfeit coin in his possession, the charge being intent to utter (circulate) forged currency. The judge sent him to prison for six months.

1861   James Jowitt, a habitual housebreaker, was found guilty of burglary at the Sheffield home of Mr James Torr and sentenced to death. He was executed at York some three weeks later.

1864   John Lyon stood in the dock charged with having placed a substance that gave off sulphurous fumes on a doorstep, which had been responsible for the death of a young child named Anne Elizabeth Foster and had seriously affected the health of a number of other children. He admitted the charge but claimed that it had never been his intention to harm any child. The chemical, which was never fully identified, had been intended for the little girl's parents and had been smeared across the step after an argument between the two families. The jury accepted Lyon's story and he was eventually sentenced to two months' imprisonment for manslaughter.

1847   Susannah Jagger (aged 60) was discovered dead on the Rotherham to Rawmarsh turnpike road, near Aldwarke Bar. She had been attacked during the early morning and her throat had been cut from ear to ear. Samuel Linley, the man she had been living with, had been seen and clearly identified as her attacker. According to witnesses, he had been drunk at the time and the two had been having a fierce argument when suddenly before anyone was able to run to her aid he knocked her to the ground and slashed her with a knife. He claimed that he had been severely provoked and that the drink had caused temporary insanity. He had not intended to do her any harm. At his trial the jury was unmoved: he was sentenced to death.

Old Yorkshire Beliefs, Omens and Sayings

When cursed by witchcraft take a necklace of dragon's blood and wear it close about the neck for four weeks and one day. All spells and curses made will then be rendered ineffective. But beware: if the wearer removes the blood too soon, all will come to pass before the next new moon.

1632   William Vickers committed suicide by walking into the River Don at Doncaster. His reason for killing himself is not recorded, but the coroner stated in his report '. . . he hath neither goodes, chattels, landes nor tenement to our knowledge', which in a macabre way was fortunate, as the goods of a suicide were forfeit to the crown. The act of suicide was seen as both a sin and a crime. If William Vickers had been wealthy he would have impoverished his family, and everything he possessed, including his clothes, would have been seized. Furthermore, had he used a weapon or a vehicle such as a cart to bring about his death, then that, known as a deodand, would have been sold and the money passed to the church to be used for a pious purpose, whatever that meant. This practice continued until 1846.

31 MAY **1838** This day brought a report of a brutal murder at Eckington. The victim, Mr Henderson, was found horrifically murdered in a backyard after a fight with a neighbour, John Guest. The uppermost part of his head had been sliced cleanly away, revealing the brain, and death had been instant, according to the examining surgeon. At the inquest, witnesses identified John Guest as having wielded the weapon that did the killing but none could explain why the fight had taken place. He was sent for trial at the Assize Court.

JUNE

✠

A sixteenth-century woodcut of a witches' coven.

1 June   **1918**   Eliza Ann Brook – Lily to her friends – liked a drink. Three times separated from husband Thomas over a three-year period, she sought him out on this day to try and set up a fourth reconciliation. Driven by drink, she managed to find him at around midday, at his father's house. The two argued. Thomas had no intention of trying to set aside their differences and told her to leave. Lily lost her temper and began shouting and swearing, calling him names. Neighbours began to gather in the street as the argument escalated, until her one-time father-in-law, determined to put an end to the fight, pushed his way into the room and with a single blow knocked her to the floor. Lily took the hint: screaming abuse at both men she stormed out into the street and ran into Doncaster. Here, on Frenchgate, she joined up with Ben Rowbottom, a man she had lived with intermittently while apart from her husband. The two discussed her confrontation over a few drinks in a number of public houses and began a drinking spree that took them into early evening. At 7 p.m. she was seen in the River Don screaming for help, watched by her drinking partner, who made no attempt to save her. An hour later she was pulled to the bank, dead. But did she jump or was she pushed – and if so, by whom?

2 June   **1831**   An inquest opened at the Bazaar Hotel, Sheffield Moor, on the body of an unnamed infant killed in an explosion at a lodging house. Elizabeth Platt, husband John Platt and the child were pulled from the remnants of the house in which they lived after much of the back kitchen had been ripped apart by an explosion at around 11 p.m. The mother of the dead child was found to have placed a stone bottle, containing a gallon of home-made liquor which she was trying to ferment, inside the oven attached to the fireplace. Tragically for the family, it slipped her mind that she had put it there, and after several hours of intense heat generated by the fire it exploded. The cast-iron oven was smashed to pieces, all the windows blown out and severe damage done to the external walls. Husband John's knee was fractured and the calf muscle of his right leg torn off, Elizabeth sustained significant bruising along much of her body, and the baby, who had been laid in front of the fire, was completely immersed in the boiling liquor and died within hours.

3 June   **1841**   A shocking tragedy took place in Rotherham as a railway engine overturned when its axle snapped. Engineman Joseph Bates and stoker John Richardson were killed instantly.

4 June   **1817**   The *Sheffield Mercury* carried a report of a brutal murder. William King beat his wife, Sarah, to death with a poker at 6.30 a.m. Neighbours heard her screams and shouts for help and gathered in the yard at the back of the house. Only John Goodlad, a scissorsmith who lived further down the terrace, plucked up enough courage to break through the back door, but King met him on the stairs still wielding the poker. Unarmed, Goodlad ran to the nearest neighbour's house and seizing their poker returned to the yard, where a vicious poker fight developed outside the house. King soon found that John Goodlad was no slouch when it came to fencing, regardless of the weapon, and he was quickly disarmed and subsequently taken away, while the mutilated body of his wife was carried from the house. Magistrates referred King to the County Assizes to stand trial for murder.

1841 An inquest opened on this day into the tragic death of Ann Turton. Ann was a young woman who had shown no outward signs of depression but had, after eating her evening meal, calmly walked down the cellar steps of her landlord's house, rigged a rope among the rafters and, jumping off a stool, hanged herself. The coroner recorded a verdict of suicide while temporarily insane.

5 June

1831 Sheffield man Edward Greenbank was sentenced to death after being found guilty of two indictments for uttering forged notes. After Greenbank made a confession in his prison cell, the sentence was later commuted to transportation for life.

6 June

1836 Daniel Hague (aged 18) and George Froggatt were sentenced to death after a 7-hour trial for the violent assault and rape of Harriet Hopkinson (aged 18) at Attercliffe in April. The jury also returned a guilty verdict on a second charge of rape during the same month on an unnamed woman in Sheffield. Daniel Hague, it appeared, had been the instigator in both attacks, but only Harriet had the courage to take the stand. She told the court that she had been attacked after leaving her father's house on Attercliffe common at around 7 p.m. Three men had followed her as she crossed the swing-bridge over the canal at Attercliffe on her way to meet a friend. After passing her by, before she had reached the other side, they turned the bridge to prevent her stepping off it and attacked her. Daniel Hague, she told the court, had produced a knife and threatened her life. Fortunately, her resistance and loud screams brought help in the shape of two young men who had been walking along the canal side before the third man was able to become involved and her attackers ran off. Unhappily for them, she knew their names and was later able to identify them.

7 June

1853 Notorious horse-thief John Wedd, alias John Weed Hudson, was returned to Doncaster after being apprehended in London when his face was recognised from a wanted poster. Williamson Eddes, a Doncaster police constable, had been called to a farm on the edge of town some two years earlier to investigate the theft of a brown mare from Sharpe's Farm. The farmer identified Wedd, whom he knew, as the thief, but police initially believed this identification to be flawed. They knew that John Wedd had been transported to Australia for exactly the same crime in March of 1847. It was some time before the authorities in Australia were able to confirm that Wedd had indeed arrived at the penal colony later that same year but had escaped in 1850. Diligent police work then traced him back to the Midlands and finally to Doncaster where he had formed a partnership

8 June

with one Jersey Joe, alias Joseph Hanson. Here, the police struck lucky: the same man had been arrested some months before for stealing a horse from another Doncaster farmer by the name of Rich. Questioning of Jersey Joe produced more information, and then an advertisement in a Warwickshire newspaper – advertising a mare for sale – pointed PC Eddes in the right direction. The mare was recovered, but Wedd made good his escape to the capital, where he stayed until finally run to earth three weeks later. Magistrates referred him to the Assizes, where he was sentenced to death or life transportation. He chose the latter.

9 June   **1854**   Reported on this day was the death of 17-year-old Henry Athorpe, son of J.C. Athorpe of Dinnington Hall. Serving as a midshipman on board the *Odin*, he had been killed during the naval attack on Gamla Carleby, Gulf of Finland.

10 June   **1860**   A grim tale was related to a Sheffield inquest. Ten-year-old Catherine Rebecca Marshall had been found dead at her father's paper mill at Owlerton. The unfortunate girl's crinoline had become entangled in a winding shaft as she walked past, dragging her into the body of the machine where she was dreadfully mangled.

11 June   **1862**   The village of Masbrough was reeling from the shock of discovering that the sexton of St Philip's Cemetery, Isaac Howard, had been caught in the act of disinterring the dead from their graves. Found guilty at his trial, he was sentenced to three months' imprisonment. Just when everyone thought the problem had disappeared the Revd J. Livesey, the incumbent of the same church, was arrested. Before Rotherham magistrates, he pleaded guilty to having falsified the entry in the register of the interment of a Joseph Greatorex. Just why he had done so was not explained, but nevertheless he shared a similar fate to his sexton, being committed to prison for three weeks.

12 June   **1861**   James Windle stood before Sheffield magistrates charged with the attempted murder of his lover, Sarah Liversidge, a married woman. The two had been carrying on an affair throughout much of 1860, but then, suspecting that she was involved with another man, he had put poison, believed to be arsenic, in her food. The court found no evidence to refute the charge and sent him to the Assizes, where he was eventually found guilty and sentenced to life imprisonment at York.

13 June   **1837**   Completed on this day was the work of laying lead pipes to carry fresh water to Sepulchre Gate, Doncaster. The project was considered a great achievement, beneficial for both the environment and public health.

14 June   **1858**   Given royal assent on this day was an Act to abolish Sheffield's Scotland Street prison and other debtors' prisons with effect from 1 August.

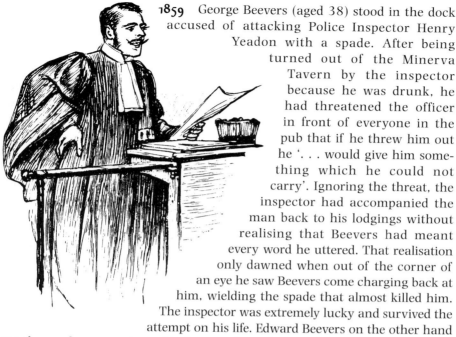

15 June

1859 George Beevers (aged 38) stood in the dock accused of attacking Police Inspector Henry Yeadon with a spade. After being turned out of the Minerva Tavern by the inspector because he was drunk, he had threatened the officer in front of everyone in the pub that if he threw him out he '. . . would give him something which he could not carry'. Ignoring the threat, the inspector had accompanied the man back to his lodgings without realising that Beevers had meant every word he uttered. That realisation only dawned when out of the corner of an eye he saw Beevers come charging back at him, wielding the spade that almost killed him. The inspector was extremely lucky and survived the attempt on his life. Edward Beevers on the other hand was less so: he was sentenced to five years' penal servitude.

Old Yorkshire Beliefs, Omens and Sayings

16 June

You must turn money over in your pocket when first you see the new moon and you will never be poor, and if you have money in your pocket when you hear the first cuckoo, it will stay with you through the year.

17 June

1863 Edwin Hides and Henry Light, both engravers, were sentenced to four years in prison after being caught at their Sheffield workshop creating forged American 'greenbacks' (dollar bills), which they intended to ship to the American continent for possible use by the Confederacy against the Union.

18 June

1787 Some said Barnsley blacksmith Samuel Truelove was a lucky man. After taking a blunderbuss from his smithy and, in front of witnesses, firing it at one John Fish, who was killed instantly, he calmly turned away and walked back to his blacksmith's shop as if nothing untoward had taken place. The luckless Mr Fish had been ordered by Barnsley magistrates to begin demolishing a number of dilapidated shops and houses, of which Truelove's smithy had been one. Truelove in turn had objected to the order but had been ignored. Shooting John Fish, whose body was found to be riddled with more than fifty pieces of shot, as he sat astride the roof of one of these buildings stripping off the tiles, had been his final protest. Although Truelove was found guilty by the court, his reasons for killing the innocent and undefended demolition worker were accepted, and he was sentenced to two years' imprisonment.

19 June   **1866** William Henry Turner was sentenced to death for the brutal murder of his infant son during a fit of anger. The jury at his trial refused to accept his defence that he had acted while temporarily insane and had not intended to kill the child. But Turner did go insane while in prison and the sentence was accordingly commuted to life.

20 June   **1864** Thomas Smith was arrested in Sheffield and brought before magistrates on a charge of stealing three sheep from a Thrybergh farm. Known locally as a thief, he had been in trouble before for stealing livestock. It was to count against him at his eventual trial: sent to the Assize Court, he was sentenced to be transported for a period of not less than twelve years.

21 June   **1861** Sheffield prizefighter Thomas Thorpe was killed by a series of blows to the head during an illegal fight outside the city. Thomas Holland, the other boxer in the ring, was arrested at the fight's conclusion and charged with murder. In court that charge was changed to manslaughter and a lengthy trial ended with Holland's being found guilty.

1909 James Holland was sentenced to five years' imprisonment after being found guilty of attempted murder. After an argument at home he had taken a hammer from the coal shed and tried to beat his wife, Mary, to death.

1860 An inquest opened at the Prince of Wales Hotel, Masbrough, into the unfortunate death of William Dixon. After a night spent in the Little Bridge Inn on Rawmarsh Road, where the man had consumed a considerable amount of alcohol, he had decided to shorten his walk home by crossing the railway lines, a habit he had perfected over the years. Regrettably, it seems that he had forgotten about the midnight mail train, which ran him down, killing him outright.

1834 Robert Colder (aged 28) pleaded guilty to having returned from transportation before the expiration of the term of his sentence. The judge told him at his trial that the offence was a capital one: the unforgiving sentence was therefore death.

1623 Jane Blomeley, widow, was indicted on this day for practising witchcraft and sorcery upon her neighbour Frances Craven of Doncaster, hence bringing about her death. The jury returned a guilty verdict and the 'witch' was burned to death a week later.

A sixteenth-century woodcut of a witch meeting the devil.

26 June **1835** *Highway Robbery at Attercliffe*. William Corker and Walter Burkenshaw stood in the dock at Sheffield's courthouse, accused of having attacked and robbed Henry Swinden – whose wife had been murdered the previous week – of £4 17s 6d, all in half-crowns. The accused had lain in wait for Swinden, having been tipped off about the amount of silver he was expected to be carrying that night. The money represented the total proceeds of a savings club which Swinden had that day withdrawn, and which was much needed in light of his wife's sad death. The magistrates sent the two to stand trial at the Winter Assizes.

27 June **1860** A dreadful accident was reported in *the Rotherham and Masbrough Advertiser*. Thomas Cavill (aged 60) had travelled from Sheffield to Rotherham to meet his daughter, who was due to arrive at the railway station on the 6 p.m. train from Castleton. After watching the train arrive and leave without his daughter and waiting a further half-hour just in case she had caught an earlier train and was somewhere in the station, he decided to return to Sheffield. Misunderstanding the timetable, he walked on to the wrong platform and, hearing the engine driver blow his whistle, ran to board the train, which began to leave. Grasping the handle of the carriage door, he managed to get his right foot on to the step, but being unable to raise his left foot, he let go and fell between train and platform. He was crushed to death beneath the wheels of the guard's van.

28 June **1847** The *Sheffield and Rotherham Independent* reported that the body of inspector Wakefield had been discovered in his own home shot through the head. One of Sheffield's most respected and successful policemen, it had initially been thought that he had been murdered, and as a result a number of potential suspects had been rounded up and questioned at Sheffield police headquarters. Further investigations however, revealed that far from being a case of murder the inspector had committed suicide. His wife admitted that their marriage had been stormy, to say the least, and that he had threatened to kill himself after the two had argued violently. The weapon used was indentified as his, one that he normally kept in a cabinet drawer. At the inquest evidence was presented that convinced the coroner that no other person had been involved and that the policeman had killed himself while suffering from temporary insanity.

29 June **1891** Mary Braithwaite of Pogmoore stood in the dock accused of murdering her child using poison, and then attempting suicide using the same substance. Obviously she survived to stand trial and the court found her guilty but insane.

30 June **1858** The murder was reported of Henry Jowitt, a Sheffield grinder, found beaten to death after a row with two men. The men, Charles Musgrave and Samuel Bennett, were eventually caught after witnesses came forward to put names to faces. At their trial, the judge overturned the charge of wilful murder, finding the two guilty of aggravated manslaughter.

JULY

Doncaster Corn Exchange.
(Doncaster Archives)

1 JULY   1839   Not satisfied with one wife, Sheffield man Benjamin Holmes (aged 38) married a second. Notwithstanding the fact that he had passed himself off as a widower, his first wife, Mary, was hale and hearty when he walked up the aisle to marry Grace Hirst, a young woman he had met in Leeds. He claimed later that Grace had stolen his heart, and he had proposed to and married her within 24 hours of meeting her. It was an impulse marriage, he told the court, after his arrest less than a day after wedding his new bride. The judge had little sympathy and sent him off to the Australian penal colonies for seven years.

2 JULY   1836   Edward Barr pleaded guilty to two indictments of forgery. He had been caught attempting to pass forged and fictitious orders on the Treasury. Had his previous record been unblemished and these only isolated instances then his sentence might have been a little more lenient, despite the fact that the offence itself was considered very serious. As it was, investigations had proved that he had been systematically carrying out fraud for over four years and his record was in fact very far from being unblemished. In that time, it transpired that he had forged some 250 fictitious Treasury notes. He was therefore sentenced to one year's hard labour, to be followed by transportation for life and a place in a chain gang.

3 JULY   1861   A most dreadful fatality occurred in Sheffield after gunpowder and other combustibles were hurled through the window of a house occupied by George Wastnidge. A fender-grinder, he had refused to join the union and had continued to work for rates of pay below those that the union members had agreed. Luckily for him he survived, but for his lodger, a Mrs Bridget O'Rourke, it was a very different story. Trapped in her upstairs room, she was unable to get out of the burning building and suffered horrific burns to much of her body before rescuers could get to her. She lived for some weeks afterwards but eventually succumbed to her terrible injuries. Fellow fender-grinder James Thompson was arrested within hours of the attack and Sheffield magistrates sent him for trial at the Assizes.

4 JULY   1838   At about 2 p.m. after a morning of intense heat, the sky over Barnsley had darkened and a terrific thunderstorm broke. Beginning at Crane Moor and extending to Eastfield, Berrymoor Moor End, Noblethorpe, Stainborough and Thurgoland, the rain eventually turned to hailstones, many of which were measured at over 2in in diameter and caused extensive damage. Crops were destroyed, windows smashed, and where the hail turned to rain it washed away cattle and finally caused a breach in the dam at Stainborough. At Moor End pit, Dodworth, forty children were about to leave the coalface as the afternoon shift changed. As they opened the door of the 'day hole' through which they had to pass to reach the surface, they were suddenly met by a wall of water. Fourteen of them managed to climb into a long slit that had been cut into the wall, which saved their lives. The other twenty-six were swept back through the door they had just opened and drowned.

Opposite: Queens Street, Barnsley, *c.* 1910. *(Brian Elliott Collection)*

1841 A tragedy occurred on this day at the launching of a new boat, the *John and William*, from Masbrough boatyard. A 70-ton, clinker-built, sloop-rigged boat, she was intended to work the River Don, the Humber estuary and the east coast. A huge crowd gathered along Forge Lane for the launch and in keeping with tradition all the small boys in the crowd were allowed to board the boat and ride the slip as it was launched. As men began to strike away the supports and the boat began its steep descent into the water, all these young children ran to one side to peer over and watch the splash as the boat left the stocks. This single movement had devastating consequences. Because this particular boat was larger than the normal canal boat, Chambers' yard built it 7ft from keel to deck, with bulwarks (the boat's sides, above deck level) projecting above that, instead of the usual 5ft 6in. This meant the launch had been angled more obliquely. As the boat hit the water, the shift in weight caused by the children, coupled with the additional height of the boat, caused it to become unstable and slip into a roll from which it could not recover. All on deck were first thrown into the water, then trapped beneath the vessel as it rolled on top of them. Had the boat been built without bulwarks, then most of the children would have survived. As it was, these acted as a fence that enclosed them and trapped them under the water. Hundreds dived into the dock and, believing that the boat was resting on the bottom of the canal, began to drive a hole into

5 JULY

the hull using axes. It was a costly mistake: as the axes broke into the hull, air
was forced out and the boat settled on to the bed of the canal, preventing any
further hope of rescue for those still held on its deck. Fifty children drowned,
almost half from Rotherham's only public school – boys who had played truant
for the thrill of watching the launch.

A nineteenth-century
boatyard, similar to
that at Masbrough.

Below: A woodcut of
the Rotherham boat
disaster. *(Rotherham
Archives and Local
Studies)*

1835 Ex-soldier William Stenton stood in the dock after being arrested on a charge of highway robbery. Armed with a pistol, he had lain in wait for Henry Pinder outside the Bird-in-the-Hand public house and attacked him on the road, stealing the food he had bought that day and the remains of his week's pay. Pinder, badly beaten but alive, had made his way back to the night watch. John Richardson, who was on duty that night, told the court that as a part of his duty he made it a point to observe Pinder as he passed him by each night and on the night of the attack he had, as usual, watched the hapless man leave the city. Some distance behind him he had also seen the prisoner, Stenton. Despite the lack of light he had been able to see enough of the man to recognise his features. The man he had seen, he told the court, now stood in the dock. This was evidence enough for the court, and William Stenton was sent to prison with hard labour.

6 JULY

1868 Joseph Beardshaw, a furnaceman of Brightside, Joseph English, a joiner of Carbrook, and Matthew Cutts, unemployed of Barnsley, were all arraigned before magistrates at Barnsley's courthouse, charged with the murder of Lord Wharncliffe's gamekeeper. George Thirkill, the keeper in question, had managed his lordship's game for a number of years and had been tipped off about a group of poachers intending to raid fields at Pilley. After lying in wait until the early hours of the morning he had surprised the group as they set their nets, but in the struggle that ensued had been shot dead. Police had

7 JULY

Cheapside, Barnsley, in the 1900s. *(Brian Elliott Collection)*

quickly rounded up the known poaching gangs in and around Barnsley, and within hours the finger of suspicion pointed firmly towards the men now in the dock. Magistrates sent them for trial and in the intervening period a fourth arrest, that of Joseph Gregory, was made. The court was unable to identify just which of the four had fired the fatal shot, so that when the verdict of guilty was announced, some six months later, none were sentenced to death. However, Joseph English, the man the court believed to have fired the fatal bullet, was singled out for harsher treatment than the rest and sent to prison for ten years.

8 JULY **1832** Sheffield Board of Health announced that cholera had struck the city. Despite warnings and precautions, over the next four months it claimed 402 lives.

9 JULY **1912** Two hours after King George V and Queen Mary had taken tea on the lawn of Conisbrough Castle on route to Wentworth Woodhouse, thirty-five men were killed in the south district of Cadeby colliery during a mine inspection. The dead included the mine inspector and most of the colliery officials who had gone down to the coalface that morning. A few hours later, as mine rescuers were arriving below ground, a series of further explosions killed another fifty-two miners.

10 JULY **1837** Sergeant Fox was dismissed from the Doncaster police force after it had been discovered that an amount of 3s 6d, intended for his constables in payment for extra duties they had undertaken during celebrations to mark the coronation of the new queen, Victoria, had been embezzled by him. An investigation had revealed that, while the money had never been paid out to those for whom it had been intended, a portion of the amount had been spent by the good sergeant.

PC George Sharp (left) and a fireman, 1925. *(Rotherham Archives and Local Studies)*

11 JULY **1916** The bodies of Barnsley couple John Jones (aged 37) and Vera Hellewell (aged 18) were discovered at Barmby Hall Farm, Cawthorne, lying beside each other, both having taken poison in a Romeo and Juliet-style suicide pact. At the inquest the court was told that they had committed suicide because they felt they could never be together in life.

1859 An unusual case came before Barnsley magistrates when Peter Burns was brought before the bench charged with concealing an infirmity that would incapacitate him from serving as a soldier. According to the evidence of the recruiting sergeant, the young man had told him that he had never tried to enlist before. It transpired after his acceptance that Mr Burns had made a habit of enlisting in order to obtain the money paid to anyone joining the ranks. Prior to his attempt in Barnsley he had been discharged as unfit for service from the West Yorks Militia. Magistrates agreed with the sergeant's assessment that it could only be deemed as taking money under false pretences. He was therefore sent to the house of correction for two months.

12 July

Old Yorkshire Cures
To cure a wart, you must first rub it with raw meat and then bury the meat in the garden, or use the slimy underpart of a black snail. The snail must then be pinned to a rowan tree.

13 July

1889 Tragedy struck on this day at Barnsley. Without warning and with no apparent motive, young Mary Braithwaite fed her baby arsenic, then killed herself by drinking a similar poison.

14 July

1855 Thomas Jackson was pronounced guilty on this day of the manslaughter of fellow soldier Private George Lewis of the 7th Hussars. After a fierce argument at the Sheffield army barracks he had shot the man dead. Jackson was sentenced to be transported beyond the seas for the remainder of his life.

15 July

1859 Patrick McKay (aged 28), Margaret McKay (30), John Shaw (20), John Williams (48) and Catherine Leonard (19) appeared in court charged with coining four half-crowns in Sheffield. The three men were found guilty and sentenced to up to eight years in prison.

16 July

1827 *Almost eaten by a lion in Barnsley.* As Jonathon Wilson stood looking at Wallace the lion in his cage at Wombwell menagerie, he incautiously placed his hand upon the bottom of the den. Without warning the lion sprang at him, seizing his arm with its claws and dragging it into the cage. As keepers fought to push the lion back he tore the man's arm to pieces. The ill-advised Wilson died eight days later from his injuries.

17 July

1914 A report of the inquest into a triple murder held at the Council Chamber at the Rawmarsh Council Offices appeared in the *Rotherham Advertiser*. Twenty-four hours earlier Emily Liversidge had awoken in the early hours of the morning and after making a fire in the kitchen had calmly sat at the table and written a short note to her husband. As daylight filtered through the windows she returned to the bedroom clutching two cut-throat razors. Waking her young son, Edgar, she sent him back downstairs with the

18 July

TRIPLE TRAGEDY AT RAWMARSH.

Mother Kills Three Children.

PATHETIC FAREWELL NOTE.

FATHER'S SHOCKING DISCOVERY.

A TERRIBLE SPECTACLE.

FULL STORY AND INQUEST.

A shocking domestic tragedy was enacted at Rawmarsh during the early hours of Thursday morning, when a woman named Emily Liversidge murdered her three children by cutting their throats with a razor. A fourth child was also attacked, but though her throat was cut, the injury was not really serious.

Immediately after the attack on her children the woman appears to have gone into her own bedroom and there attempted to commit suicide. She was discovered there later, but although the wound in her throat was a terrible gash, life was not extinct.

THE VICTIMS.

The victims of the tragedy are:—
Emma Liversidge, aged six years.
Jessie Liversidge, aged three years.
Belinda Liversidge, aged six months.

These three children were all dead when discovered.

The fourth child, Rose, aged ten years, had also been attacked and her throat cut, but the injury had not been sufficient to end her life.

The mother herself was also alive at the time the tragedy was discovered.

The discovery was made by the father of the children, Arthur Liversidge, a miner, who is employed at the Silverwood colliery. He had been working on the night shift, and returned to his home, 101, Green Lane, Rawmarsh, shortly after seven o'clock on Thursday morning.

THE MOTHER'S NOTE.

At the entrance of the yard he was met by his twelve-year-old son, Edgar, who told him he was to look on the cornice for a note from his mother.

where she made a fire. Afterwards she appears to have secured two of her husband's razors, and, taking them upstairs, attacked the children as they were sleeping in their beds.

"I LOVE MY BABIES."

When the police entered the house Mrs. Liversidge was found lying on her left side on the floor of the front bedroom. She was bleeding from a wound in the throat. During the time her wounds were being dressed the woman made a rambling statement:—

"Mamma's done it," she murmured pathetically. "I love my babies. I wish I could die."

There is no apparent motive for the crime, and it is only to be attributed to a sudden fit of madness.

The boy, Edgar, is the only child who can tell a story of the happenings preceding the tragedy. He states that his mother roused him very early. It was broad daylight when she came into the room and awakened him, saying "Get up, love, and go downstairs. Unlock the door, and pull the blind up. The fire is made. Let dad in when he comes."

The boy replied: "Let me get into bed again," but his mother was firm and answered "No, go downstairs."

AWAITING HIS FATHER.

The lad obeyed and went downstairs to await the coming of his father. He did not see what happened, and had no knowledge of the tragedy until his father came home and made the discovery. He remembers his mother instructing him to tell his father to look for the note on the cornice, but beyond that he can throw no light on the tragedy.

Mr. Liversidge was equally unable to explain the terrible event. He was frightfully upset by

instruction that he was to wait for his father returning from the pit and show him the note, which she had sealed in an envelope and left on the mantelpiece. Waiting until she was sure the boy had gone into the kitchen, she then lifted the youngest of her four daughters, 6-month-old Belinda, from her cot, laid the infant on a small table beneath the window and proceeded to cut her throat. In an almost mechanical manner, she followed this murder with that of her other daughters, all asleep in a back room. She attacked each in turn with a razor, slashing at their throats, leaving them where they lay until, satisfied that she had killed all four, she used the razor on herself. In fact one daughter survived. When husband Arthur arrived at the house on Green Lane after his night shift at Silverwood colliery Edgar, the son deliberately omitted from the orgy of killing, was unaware of just what had taken place and simply did as his mother had asked. The note was short:

Dear Arthur, keep and bless Edgar dearly, as you love us all. Send for mother, Aunt Belinda and Mrs Platt. Love for Horace and Emily and yourself. I have gone mad.

19 JULY

The report of the triple murder.
(Rotherham Advertiser)

1915 A report of an ill-fated day out appeared on this day. William Briggs, home on leave from the army, borrowed a bicycle and rode out to Tickhill to enjoy the warm weather. Stopping outside the small town, he wandered into a pea field, sat down with a paper bag and proceeded to fill it with peas. Opposite where he sat, farmer Edward Fisher, incensed by the theft of his crop, shouted at the young soldier to leave his peas alone. When shouts appeared to make no impression he raised his shotgun to his shoulder and fired both barrels. The soldier took the full force of the blast, with shot peppering his legs, head, back, arms and thighs. Struggling to regain his feet he managed to escape and freewheel back into Tickhill. Here a surgeon removed the shot and saved his life. The farmer, who was duly arrested, told the jury at his trial that he had never believed the shot would carry that far and thought the young man was out of danger's reach. He was sent to prison for one month.

1865 There were reports of serious riots in Rotherham as recent election results were announced. Crowds had been gathering all day along High Street, most wearing orange ribbons in support of radical candidates Milton and Beaumont. As it became known that the Conservatives had polled well, questions were shouted from the crowd and rumours began to spread that the vote had somehow been rigged. By early evening a full-blown riot was in progress and a detachment of hussars formed a line and charged the crowd, scattering them through the town and eventually cornering a large number inside the Lion Yard. Police then attempted to capture the ringleaders but were fought off by men wielding sticks and hurling stones. One man was run through four times by an officer of hussars, and many others sustained sword cuts and bad bruising before the streets were finally cleared.

20 JULY

1913 Persistence was a trait John Badgers was said to have possessed almost to excess. At his appearance in court for attempting to commit suicide while being held in Conisbrough police station, magistrates were told that this had been the third attempt he had made since being arrested. On the first occasion, he had hanged himself by his belt from the cell window, but had been cut down by officers and his life saved. The second instance, in the same cell, had been a further attempt at hanging, using his shirt as a rope, but again he was delivered. The third attempt, and the one that had brought him to court, had involved the use of his own fists: found on the floor of the same cell, he had attempted to beat himself to death. Magistrates decided to send him for trial at the Assizes – if he could be kept alive long enough.

21 JULY

1871 On this day George Bishop and his brother were cutting grass in a field at the back of their father's house in Dore, Sheffield, when a quarrel broke out between the two. Hearing raised voices, their father stormed out of the house and, pulling the two boys apart, struck George and told him in no uncertain terms to get on with the job in hand. Greatly irritated and somewhat discomfited by the sudden intervention, George stepped back and aimed a swinging blow at his father with the long-handled scythe he held in his right hand. The point of the scythe entered the older man's body just below the left shoulder blade and exited through the chest; their father was dead as he hit the ground. At his subsequent trial George Bishop was found guilty of manslaughter.

22 JULY

1782 Francis Fearn was executed for the brutal murder of Sheffield watchmaker Nathan Andrews. Jealous of Nathan's pocket-watch, he invented a story about a watch club that had been formed at Bradfield and invited the watchmaker

23 JULY

A gibbeted body, hung by a chain to deter others.

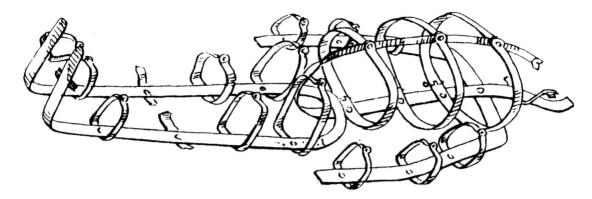

Chains like those used to gibbet Francis Fearn.

to join, with the sole purpose of showing his watch to the club members, a common enough practice intended to stimulate interest in watches and create selling opportunities. Mr Andrews readily accepted the invitation. As the two men neared Bradfield, Fearn shot the watchmaker in the back, stabbed him and finally beat him to death with a hedge stake. Unluckily for the killer, though, he had been seen in Nathan Andrews' company on the day of the murder. After the execution his body was hung from a gibbet at Loxley, where it remained for twenty-five years.

24 JULY   1904   Doncaster's court minutes record that Noah Myers, shown only as a minor, was found guilty of stealing three pennies from William Thomas (aged 5) and sentenced to three strokes of the birch.

25 JULY   1859   A sad story of unrequited love unfolded before an inquest at Barnsley on this day. Jane King (aged 18), a domestic servant from Hoyland, met a young man, Charles Totty, and fell head over heels in love. The two were seen together for the best part of a year before Totty, described by the *Barnsley Chronicle* as being 'rough and coarse in manners', ended the relationship. Jane King was utterly devastated, having harboured the thought that one day the two would marry, and ran away to Lancashire to try and put the whole sad and sorry tale behind her. There she discovered that she was pregnant. After some three or four months, she returned to South Yorkshire and tried to re-establish contact with the man with whom she was still deeply in love. She kept the pregnancy secret, taking a domestic job at the Nag's Head Inn, near Barnsley. After a further three months, her condition became more difficult to conceal and her employers discovered her secret. This prompted her to write a letter to Charles Totty arranging a meeting, probably to tell him of her circumstances and hoping for marriage. But it seems that Totty had no intention of helping her out: he refused to marry her and after walking around Wosborough Dale with her until 3 a.m. left her to walk back to her lodgings. Desperate, depressed and friendless, she walked as far as Beckside Pond at Hoyland, where she removed her pink-trimmed bonnet, netted collar, gloves and – last of all – the brooch bought a few weeks earlier, inside which she had intended to place a portrait of

the man she loved. Then the forsaken young girl drowned herself. The coroner returned a verdict that Jane King had drowned in a pond, having committed suicide under depression of spirits caused by the heartless conduct of Mr Charles Totty.

1910 After an argument with his lover, John Courtney, a Doncaster labourer, took an axe from an outhouse and proceeded to strike her about the head and face. Believing that he had murdered her he then fled, avoiding arrest for almost three weeks. Fortunately for her – but less so for him – the victim, Elizabeth Dukes, survived and was able to tell police exactly what had happened. Courtney went to prison for seven years.

26 July

1900 Charles Backhouse (aged 22) and his brother Frederick (aged 19) entered the dock before Mr Justice Ridley at the Quarter Assizes, charged with the murder of Police Constable John William Kew, whose beat covered their Swinton home. The brothers were well known to the police, and in particular to PC Kew, for various acts of petty theft. PC Kew had served a summons on Frederick for an assault upon his brother Charles's wife, and when the defendant had not turned up in court on the due date, he had been fined 40s and sentenced to one month's imprisonment. It meant little to the brothers and some days after the court hearing they bought a revolver and nine bullets and began to threaten people in the Swinton neighbourhood. Constable Kew was sent to investigate. As he arrived in Piccadilly, he saw the two men, stopped

27 July

them and informed them that he was going to search them. At that point Charles Backhouse drew the revolver and shot the constable in the stomach. Seriously injured, Kew nevertheless grabbed hold of Charles and wrestled with him, forcing the gun back behind his back. It was at that juncture that the other brother seized the weapon and shot Kew in the right hip. The constable died the next day, but not before he had identified his killers. Both were found guilty of murder. Frederick, because of his age, was reprieved; Charles was hanged by executioner James Billington.

28 JULY **1861** There were celebrations in Sheffield after the arrival back in town of Daniel Dickenson. Eminent among the local criminal fraternity, he had been thought lost to the city forever after being convicted of a burglary that had gone violently wrong, with the owners of the house being brutally beaten. At his trial he had been sentenced to transportation for life. Providentially for him, his conviction was found to be unsafe and he was released from prison before his ship sailed. He was a lucky man indeed: few who were sentenced to transportation ever saw their home again.

29 JULY **1858** An inquest opened at the Green Dragon Inn, Kimberworth, into the deaths of three men at Grange Colliery. All were killed in the explosion that followed their attempt to remove a water pipe. The coroner recorded a verdict of accidental death caused by an explosion of firedamp (methane gas), with the jury adding that the work had been carried out under 'careless and inefficient management'.

30 JULY **1906** Mark Kay (24) and Joseph Beaumont (27) were killed by lightning as they sheltered from a thunderstorm under a beech tree in Wombwell Wood.

31 JULY **1886** Police Constable Austwick was found shot dead at Dodworth. After being stopped in the street by PC Austwick at around 11 p.m. for being drunk, William Murphy went home to fetch his shotgun and returned minutes later to shoot the policeman dead. The killer – with twenty-six convictions to his name, ranging from petty theft to housebreaking – had become incensed at what he believed to be police harassment, particularly from local beat bobby Austwick. For the next five weeks he remained on the run from police before finally being cornered inside a tenement block, one of a block of three, known locally as Dyson's Cottages, where Murphy had rented the rooms under a false name. When Detective Sergeant William Lodge opened the door, it was to a room devoid of any kind of furnishings and all he saw, kneeling opposite the door through which he had entered, was William Murphy. The man levelled a shotgun at him and was about to fire when the policeman, with the aid of his trusty umbrella, knocked the gun out of his grasp and made the arrest that would make him famous. At his trial Murphy insisted that the killing of Constable Austwick had been the result of victimisation and that when he had fired the fatal shots he had been temporarily insane. This submission carried absolutely no weight with the judge or the jury, who returned a guilty verdict. Murphy was executed at York.

Police Superintendent Gower, 1912. (*Rotherham Archives and Local Studies*)

AUGUST

Window of Scotland Street Gaol, behind which many of the
city's nineteenth-century prisoners served their sentences.
(Sheffield Libraries, Archives and Local Studies)

1 AUGUST   **1859**   Another diabolical outrage at Sheffield, reported *the Rotherham and Masbrough Advertiser*. James Linley, a saw-grinder, had been shot at for the third time in a year, this time the wound proving fatal. In the two previous attempts on his life – believed to have been made with the same gun – the injuries sustained had not been serious. Sadly this third attempt, made as he sat drinking in the Crown Inn, Sheffield, had mortally wounded him in the head. Surgeons were unable to remove the ball, which had lodged 3in inside his temple, behind the right eye. The killer, having fired through a plate-glass window, had escaped after the shooting. Linley's refusal to join the trade union was believed to have been the motive for the killing.

2 AUGUST   **1850**   Joseph Eastwood (aged 23), who was on this day found guilty of stealing fowl to the value of *2s* from farmer William Maplebeck, was a serial offender who had been before the bench on numerous occasions. At his trial the judge took the view that the country would be better served if Maplebeck were ejected from it; he therefore sentenced him to seven years' transportation to the Australian penal colony.

3 AUGUST   **Old Yorkshire Beliefs, Omens and Sayings**
Spilt salt is considered an ill omen. To ward off the Devil, a pinch of salt must be cast over the right shoulder for luck, and thrown across the fireback to ward off any evil spirits.

4 AUGUST   **1795**   After an evening parade, Sheffield soldiers refused to disperse until Colonel Althorpe, their commanding officer, paid all their outstanding back-pay. This he refused, and as the soldiers remonstrated their numbers were slowly swelled by the Sheffield public, who began to gather in support. One cavalry officer, realising his colonel had lost control, drew his sabre and plunged his horse into the crowd, cutting down women and children alike. At that point as the crowd fell back, the Colonel ordered the Riot Act to be read and brought up a volunteer militia group to block off the exit to Norfolk Street. The militia fired several volleys into the fleeing mob, killing a number of them. At the inquest into the deaths held 24 hours later, the coroner returned a verdict of justifiable homicide.

5 AUGUST   **1864**   James Thompson, a cutler and sometime butcher, attempted to murder his wife, Emma. He had ill-treated her for all of the three years they had known each other, and one year after their marriage she left him. In an effort to start a new life he went to America where he stayed for nine months. On his return to Sheffield he met Emma by accident at the Sheffield fair. In an unprovoked attack he punched her in the face, and was duly arrested and sent to prison for six months. After a series of failed attempts to meet her he discovered she was staying at her mother's house. On this day, taking a knife to Sheffield Moor slaughterhouse, he had it sharpened then waited for Emma to set off to work from the house. Catching her on the street he plunged the knife into her chest and took to his heels. But the blade

Volley firing as the Sheffield crowds of 4 August would have witnessed it.

had struck a rib and Emma escaped with her life. Thompson was sentenced to life imprisonment.

1839 Chartists met in Paradise Square, Sheffield, against the wishes of magistrates, to try to agree a date for the 'sacred month', when all labour would be withdrawn for a four-week period. The meeting failed to reach agreement but decided on three days of marches, during which all working-class members were to take to the streets.

6 August

1836 A report of an inquest at Sheffield Town Hall on the body of Robert Marshall, turnkey of Scotland Street Gaol, revealed that he had died as a direct result of being assaulted by one of the prison inmates, William Newsome, who had struck out at him and knocked him to the floor. Disastrously for Marshall his head struck the ground with a greater force than his attacker had intended, and his skull was fractured. At his trial some eight months later, Newsome pleaded not guilty to wilful murder and mounted a defence of manslaughter. The jury accepted the plea and added one year to his sentence.

7 August

1892 On this day a horrific accident befell Herbert Dent (aged 19) of Braithwell. As he climbed over a hedge carrying his loaded shotgun, he slipped and his fingers caught the trigger. Both barrels were emptied into his left arm. After lying on the ground for several hours he managed to make his way

8 August

home where he was attended by a surgeon and sent to hospital. The arm was amputated but Herbert did not survive the night.

9 AUGUST **1839** The Chartist marches, agreed three days earlier despite a proclamation issued by magistrates forbidding the action, began in Sheffield. Huge crowds gathered to watch the procession of workers as they wound their way through the city streets, but as the day wore on spectators and workers slowly became one. Anger erupted into riot, forcing the authorities to call out the militia with predictable results. Running battles erupted all over the city, with considerable damage being caused to property. For the next ten days, determined not to be beaten, the Chartists held a series of torchlight meetings at Sky Edge, where they could be seen from the city below, but where they were difficult to attack. This led to even more military being brought into the city and eventually the torchlight meetings were stopped. But the riots continued, though somewhat muted, and in total over eighty people were arrested.

View of Sky Edge, Sheffield, 1844. *(Sheffield Libraries, Archives and Local Studies)*

1915 On this day Walter Marriott hanged for the murder of his wife, Nellie. Walter claimed that during a violent fight at their Barnsley home she had attacked him with a bread knife, and that as they fought in the kitchen, she had been accidentally stabbed in the neck. The jury, considering that 7½in of blade had penetrated Nellie's neck and chest, believed he had indeed intended to kill her. Thomas Pierrepoint carried out the execution.

10 AUGUST

1884 The body of a 6-week-old baby girl was found floating in a stream near Stainborough. She had been in the water for several days and, according to doctors, had not drowned but been beaten to death. The mother, Ann Parkin, was quickly arrested after neighbours reported her to police on reading of the discovery. They had grown suspicious after not seeing her with her newly born daughter. Although Parkin was initially sentenced to death, this was later commuted to penal servitude.

11 AUGUST

1837 Thomas Williams was executed in public in front of a huge crowd, for the murder of basket-weaver Thomas Froggatt with a billhook, which sliced off the top of his head.

12 AUGUST

1825 A report appeared in the *Sheffield Mercury* of the execution of Isaac Charlesworth before a crowd estimated at over 6,000. Guilty of highway robbery, he had been identified by witnesses who claimed to have seen him rob and assault a man named Green. At his trial the judge told the jury that there could be no doubt of Charlesworth's guilt because the weapon used in the assault had been found upon his person. But Charlesworth insisted he was innocent, calling the witnesses for the prosecution 'perjured men'.

13 AUGUST

1840 This day brought a report of an attempted murder at Rivelin Mill. Ann Law, in a fit of anger, took her daughter by the hand and threw her into the river intending that she drown. Passers-by managed to drag the little girl back to the water's edge and save her life. Sheffield magistrates sent the mother to prison for eighteen months.

14 AUGUST

1841 A deplorable case of robbery and violence happened at the home of Mr William Dyson in Ecclesfield. Joseph Turner and William Housley, who were arrested shortly after the burglary, were found to have either stolen or handled the property that had been taken. They were sentenced to be transported for fourteen years. In the same courtroom, and for a very similar crime, William Smith and James Bailey, both from Sheffield, found themselves obliged to join them on their trip abroad for ten years.

15 AUGUST

1904 John Kay was executed on this day for the murder of his lover, Jane Hurst, by John Billington, probably a relation of James Billington, the state executioner. Kay had never denied his guilt. In a full and frank confession he had told police that after living together since September 1903, she and Kay had decided to take in a lodger, a young labourer. Their financial situation had

16 AUGUST

John Kay.
*(Rotherham
Advertiser)*

been poor, since Kay had been unable to find regular work. It was a move designed to take some of this financial pressure away. The young man, whom Kay had been working with, moved into the dilapidated cottage on Sheffield Road in March. It was this decision, according to John Kay, that had proved the catalyst to murder. Within three weeks of his arrival at the cottage the young man had begun an affair with Jane Hurst that only ended after Kay found them in bed together. The lodger was of course thrown out, the pressure on their finances returned and their relationship plunged to an understandable low.

Jane sought solace in the bottle and began to embark on a series of binge-drinking sessions, which would take her all over Sheffield with the inevitable result that she began to stay away from home, probably too drunk to care, until her money ran out. At that point Kay would go off to find her and bring her back. This became a kind of routine until, in May of 1904, tired of Jane's drinking and believing her to have been unfaithful for a second time, he decided to take drastic action. In the early hours of the morning while she slept, he crept downstairs, took a hatchet from a downstairs room and returned to the bedroom, where he beat her to death. He then walked into Rotherham, where he surrendered himself to Police Sergeant Brookes in Effingham Street.

John Kay's cottage.
(Rotherham Advertiser)

1897 Joseph Robinson was executed at Armley gaol for the murder of his 24-year-old wife, Florence, in the yard of their house at Monk Bretton. Robinson was described as violent: one of his children had previously died after being snatched out of Florence's arms during a row. He had even attempted to give away another of his children. He had decided, after years of separations and reconciliations, to rid himself of the woman he believed responsible for all that ailed him. After buying a gun and a quantity of laudanum he shot her dead at the back of the house and swallowed the laudanum in an unsuccessful attempt to kill himself.

1843 A sentence of death was passed on Aaron Green and Henry Stones, the Sheffield burglars who had inflicted dreadful injuries on farm labourer Thomas Biggin in a robbery at his house at Dore in February. The two were hanged at York.

1786 A double drop involving William Sharp (aged 26) and William Bamford (aged 28) brought large crowds to York to see them executed for burglary in front of the castle, many having travelled over from South Yorkshire for the spectacle. The pair had been found guilty of the theft from a shop owned by Duncan MacDonald, a Sheffield button-maker, of horn buttons and a silver threepenny piece. Not a very profitable endeavour!

1644 Major Thomas Beaumont was marched out of Sheffield as a prisoner, after surrendering its castle to the Parliamentarian army nine days earlier. The city had fallen easily to Cromwell's army, but resistance at the castle had been fierce, albeit brief. Only the use of siege guns had forced its capitulation and then only after considerable damage had been done with the concomitant loss of life from such heavy artillery. With the castle pounded into submission, the Major had little choice but to seek terms.

1841 William Jones was fined 17s for driving his cart through Rotherham while asleep. He told the court at Rotherham that he had left the driving to a man he had picked up along the road, and had not realised that his companion had jumped off before the cart reached the town.

1887 Henry Hobson (aged 54) was hanged on this day for murdering his lover, Ada Stothard. The two had been carrying on an affair for several months. After an argument at her home in Sheffield he had seized a cut-throat razor and slashed her throat. However, unbeknown to him he had been seen by Ada's servant girl.

1847 On this day came a report of the release of all Sheffield prisoners held in the city gaol – a total of around eighty men and women – and a further seven men held at Eccleshall, after an Act of Parliament was passed which prohibited imprisonment for debts below £20.

24 August   1855 James Burke and Cormack Dunlevy were committed to York Assizes for the murder of Police Constable William Beardshaw. During a riot by Irish workers in Sheffield over working conditions and pay, the officer had attempted to disperse the crowd. Dunlevy had attacked him with a blunt instrument, possibly a stick or a stone, and had managed to beat him to the ground. Burke then joined in and Beardshaw was brutally beaten to death. Originally charged with wilful murder they could have expected to be hanged, particularly as the dead man had been a policeman. But they were lucky. The argument mounted in their defence, that they had not intended to kill him but only struck out to prevent him arresting them, was accepted by the judge. He declared the offence to be one of manslaughter and after the verdict had been read, and in light of the prosecution view that Dunlevy had been the instigator of the attack, he ordered that he be transported for fifteen years, while Burke went to prison for only twelve months.

25 August   1866 A most unlucky accident was reported today. Robert Nixon, a joiner, had just completed a job in Sheffield and was running across the city to begin his next piece of work when he lost his footing and fell in the street. The hapless woodworker had regrettably placed a chisel in the breast pocket of his overall and as he fell, the newly sharpened tool entered his chest, puncturing his heart and killing him.

26 August   1884 Joseph 'Jimmy Armhole' Laycock was executed at York for the murder of his wife. It was James Billington's first execution and he gave the condemned man a drop of 8ft 4in. He had intended a 9ft drop but when told that Laycock had attempted to cut his own throat, he reduced the fall in order to prevent the wound reopening.

27 August   1867 The frame and stump of the gibbet that had held the caged body of the executed highwayman Spence Broughton was discovered in the cellar of a house in Clifton Street, Attercliffe Common, just opposite the Yellow Lion public house. It had hung there for thirty-five years after his execution for robbing the Sheffield to Rotherham mail in 1792.

Doncaster Union Workhouse. *(Reproduced by kind permission of Doncaster Library and Information Services)*

1846 Charles Glover (aged 16), 'untimely slain': so reads the headstone of his grave in St James's Church, Norton. The youngster was attacked by a group of men and cruelly murdered outside Sheffield.

28 August

1879 This day brought reports of great floods in Mexborough, which placed much of the town under water after tremendous thunderstorms had flooded many of the surrounding fields and swollen the Don to capacity. Edward Jones was the only unfortunate victim after he fell into the canal at Swinton Bridge and was washed away. His body was not recovered until some days later.

29 August

30 August **1811** Elliott's Lozenges were advertised in the *Sheffield Mercury* as a pill to cure-all-ills. According to the testimony of Abel Tinker he had given them to his son and seen him excrete twenty-one worms. Elliotts of Huddersfield claimed they not only cleaned out the body but would also purge the blood of measles, smallpox and all skin disorders – all for the incredible price of *2d.*

31 August **1859** Spoon-buffer Jane Bunting (aged 17) of Sheffield found herself before the magistrates charged with stealing a coat belonging to apprentice John Salt from a grocer's shop. Possibly the most ineffective thief ever to stand in the dock, she had carried out the theft in broad daylight and had been seen by everyone in the shop. She had dropped the coat as she ran and was caught 10yds from the shop's back door by the grocer's porter who she almost knocked over as she tried to escape. This, according to magistrates, had been her third failed attempt at stealing and so the sentence passed was six months' hard labour. Her fourth conviction, this was also the fourth time she had been sent to prison in the last two years.

SEPTEMBER

✠

CERTIFICATE TO BE SIGNED BY
THE CHIEF BAILIFF.

I certify, that Lt. Priest

is in my Custody for Debt. He is not work-
ing, and I think him entitled to receive
Bread.

Jas. Kirk

CERTIFICATE TO BE SIGNED BY
THE PRISONER'S LAST EM-
PLOYER.

I certify, that Thos. Priest
was lately employed at Strings
by me, but is not working at present.

Geo. Priest

Nineteenth-century bread warrant,
Scotland Street Gaol.
(Sheffield Libraries, Archives and Local Studies)

1 SEPTEMBER   **1844**   William Mason, George Taylor and Richard Winker were all found guilty of riot and assault. They had been part of a group of miners who had attacked Soap House Pit after the owners had brought other labour in to take over some of their jobs. A military force had to be called out to contain the violence and regain control of the pithead. Police accused the three of being the instigators of the riot and they were subsequently found guilty and transported to Australia for fifteen years.

2 SEPTEMBER   **1791**   John Bennett was executed on this day for his part in riots that had destroyed much of Sheffield's King Street prison and released most of its prisoners. A leading player in the orchestrated attack he had also led the rioters towards the vicarage at Broomhall where they had rampaged through the house destroying a large section of the library, damaged a number of pieces of furniture beyond repair and then set hayricks alight in the adjoining fields.

3 SEPTEMBER   **1925**   Wilfred Fowler, one of the notorious Fowler gang that had terrorised much of Sheffield, was executed for the brutal murder of William Plommer. An ex-boxer, Plommer had refused to be intimidated by the Fowler brothers and their henchmen; he had even knocked one of them senseless after a run-in earlier in the year. Revenge was sought and after another fight in April in a bar, from which Wilfred Fowler was carried out unconscious, the brothers brought together a group of 'heavies'. Twenty-four hours after Wilfred's beating, his brother Lawrence and seven members of the gang arrived outside Plommer's home. Like something out of a Wild West film they called Plommer outside. Not about to be cowed into submission the ex-boxer stepped out into the street. He stood no chance. Wielding chains, clubs and knives the mob attacked him as he stepped away from his door. He died the following day as a result of his wounds.

4 SEPTEMBER   **1925**   Lawrence Fowler, the other half of the Fowler gang, had been forced to wait a further 24 hours before being allowed to follow his brother to the scaffold. He was executed on this day at 8 a.m. by Thomas Pierrepoint.

5 SEPTEMBER   **1903**   Joseph Hirst and Ephraim Beddows, Royston miners, were both found guilty of the attempted murder of Woolley Park gamekeeper Walter Davis. They had been caught poaching in the early hours of an August morning and during the fight that ensued had beaten the keeper with heavy sticks and stones, and made good their escape. But Walter Davis knew many of the men who poached in his fields. He recognised the two miners during the assault and both were arrested within days. The previous penalty for poaching with violence had been transportation. Fortunately for them the keeper survived and as transportation to Australia had ceased thirty-six years earlier, they were sent to prison for ten years' penal servitude.

6 SEPTEMBER   **1879**   The country's executioner, William Marwood, gave a lecture in Sheffield to an interested public. Over 600 people turned out to hear the man who was

responsible for refining the theory of the 'long drop', a mathematical calculation which decided the length of the drop from the scaffold needed to execute a condemned prisoner humanely, the distance being dictated by his or her weight. Prior to this scientific approach most of those hanged were slowly strangled to death. Under the new system, death was instantaneous. Unfortunately for his paying audience Marwood would not speak of his occupation, only of the Bible, the forthcoming parliamentary election and the Irish question. As the night progressed the crowd grew ever more impatient, with a number of men heckling from the back of the room, while others left, demanding a refund of their ticket price.

Executioner William Marwood.

1868   Richard Downs was found guilty of the manslaughter of Mary Sherdon. He and three other men, Samuel Wass, William Oldfield and Patrick Waldon, had attacked and raped her in Brightside Lane, Sheffield. But of the four, it was found that Downs had been the instigator of the attack and had used unnecessary violence, beating her so severely that she had later died of her injuries. He was sent to prison for life; the other three each received a twelve-month sentence.

7 SEPTEMBER

1888   *Sorrow, trouble, passion and debauchery.* A report in the *Barnsley Chronicle* recounted how Henry Hey, landlord of the Blacksmith's Arms, Millhouses, shot his domestic servant, Margaret Hill (22), in a fit of madness. Two years earlier he and his wife had decided to take over the pub and be their own bosses. On the face of it this was a good decision but ex-plasterer Henry Hey could not resist drinking away the profits. The marriage had slowly begun to disintegrate and as it did so, violence became the only means he had of settling any kind of argument. Margaret had been taken on some nine months earlier to lessen the burden. But Henry began to pay more attention to her than the business. Arriving with a bit of a history to her name, she had lived with two different men during her young life and had two children, one to each, which had begun to cause a deal of jealousy between the landlord and his good wife. She saw the servant as an interloper and a threat to her marriage, and after a particularly violent row, left to go and live with friends near by. Whether as a result of her departure or just because of the pressures of his daily life, Henry slowly went mad. By

8 SEPTEMBER

the summer he had begun to be delusional and had stopped doing any work about the place.

As September dawned it became clear to Henry's son that he was a threat to both of them, and he hid the shotgun that was normally kept behind the bar, refusing to tell his father where he had put it. But madness can be a resourceful illness and the gun was eventually found. From the moment Hey managed to get hold of it, there seemed little doubt that he would use it. Margaret Hill walked into his bedroom as he sat cradling the weapon in his arms and tried to talk him out of any notion of suicide. He immediately shot her in the side and as she sat on the bedroom floor holding her hands to the gaping wound, he shot her a second time. In his statement to police, he had told them that his intention had been to use one barrel on her and one on himself, but when the first shot failed to kill her he felt almost honour bound to use the last remaining shot to finish her off. At the inquest, held inside Hey's own pub, examining surgeon Arthur Jordan told the jury that a post-mortem had also revealed that Margaret Hill had been four months pregnant. Henry Hey was found to have been quite mad.

9 SEPTEMBER

1864 *A double drop.* Upwards of 80,000 people turned up to watch the executions of James Sargisson and Joseph Myers. Sargisson had beaten to death 26-year-old John Cooper in Roche Abbey Lane with a fence post, with the objective of stealing his watch. Myers had stabbed his wife Nancy to death with a pair of scissors.

An engraving showing a public execution.

10 SEPTEMBER

1897 On this day there occurred the shocking death of a drayman in Barnsley. Joseph Milton (aged 54) was driving his heavily laden dray through Barnsley when, in order to pick up a little speed, he whipped one of the two horses. At that precise point the horse slipped and Milton fell forward, between the rear of the horse and the dray. Frightened, the horse kicked out, catching him on the head. Milton landed in the road and all four wheels of the dray ran over his head, neck and torso. According to the doctor who tried to save his life, he had broken every rib on the right side of his body, fractured his skull, lacerated his right temple and ruptured all the organs in his abdomen, including both kidneys. He died some hours later.

1820   A report in the *Annals of Yorkshire* states that Waterloo hero John Comstive attempted to lead a division of Barnsley malcontents, mainly unemployed labourers, on to the moor between the town and Huddersfield. It was to have been a coordinated attempt at an uprising, with a large body of men from the north joining the group at a prearranged place. Unfortunately the northern uprising failed, with most of the would-be insurgents' arms, mainly pikes, being discovered by the army. The Barnsley men scattered as soon as news reached them, but Comstive and twenty-one others were captured by the King's Troop. Before their trial on a charge of high treason, which brought with it an automatic death sentence, he was asked to mediate with the group, telling them that they could all avoid execution by pleading guilty. After some discussion the deal was agreed: all were sentenced to seven years' transportation.

11 September

1862   Phoebe Mason told a court that her intended husband had, after agreeing to marry her, married a cousin in her stead and set up a public house at Crosspool, Sheffield. A sad and sorry tale of deception, duplicity and betrayal unravelled itself before Mr Justice Willes. Phoebe was only 17 years old when she had met John Furniss, who was attracted to her from that first meeting. Furniss managed to inveigle his way into her and her family's life, becoming accepted as an adopted son, eating his meals at the family hotel and

12 September

Eldon Street and Civic Hall, Barnsley, *c.* 1900. *(Brian Elliott Collection)*

The crank, often used
in Victorian prisons
as an alternative
to the treadmill.
*(Steve Jones, Wicked
Publications)*

TURN 14,500 TIMES
& PICK 1105 OAKUM
PER DAY

TURN 12,500 TIMES
PICK 6 OZ OAKUM
PER DAY.

TURN 10,500 TIMES
PER DAY.

eventually requesting the young girl's hand in marriage. But it was all a ruse: he had never intended to marry her and had been carrying on an affair with his cousin, a much wealthier woman, for a very long time. Unaware of all this subterfuge, believing she was to become the next Mrs Furniss, Phoebe began to sleep with him, a situation that continued until he realised she had become pregnant. At that point Furniss cut and ran, and married the other woman in his life. The learned judge agreed Phoebe had been abominably treated and ordered Mr Furniss to pay her £150 for breach of promise.

13 September **1862** Notorious criminal George Gouldthorpe was arrested at the Three Cranes public house in Sheffield after a trap had been laid to catch him selling stolen silver. John Slaughter, who ran a prosperous jewellery business off Sheffield's Fargate, had been approached by a young man and asked if he would be interested in buying a deal of silver, mainly cutlery. Realising almost at once that the cutlery being offered had probably been stolen and that the theft of silver cutlery from Darnall parsonage had recently been in the newspaper headlines, the jeweller put two and two together and agreed to inspect the goods. He was taken to meet Gouldthorpe the following day and shown a quantity of silver knives, spoons, forks, sugar tongs and a pocket communion service. A rough weighing told him that the market price was in the region of £5 and he agreed to meet again the next day in the Three Cranes to hand over the cash. However, in the interim Slaughter alerted Sheffield police, who subsequently arrested Gouldthorpe in a covert operation.

14 September **1887** Elizabeth Ogden (aged 8) died on this day in extremely peculiar circumstances. At 12.05 p.m., while running down Bridgegate, she fell in the street. It would have been a trifling incident, except that the school slate that Elizabeth was carrying had lost its wooden frame and as she fell her throat caught the sharp edge and she died of asphyxia.

15 September **1906** The inquest opened into the death of William Whinfield, who had been struck five times on the head with a hatchet. The unfortunate man had survived the initial attack but died ten days later after septicaemia had infected one of the wounds. The perpetrator of this brutal attack, Benjamin

Smithies, had shared lodgings with him at 75 Sheffield Road and had shown no outward signs of animosity towards him. Thirteen-year-old John Wood, who saw the attack, and his sister Matilda, who witnessed the aftermath, told the coroner that Smithies came home after a night out at around 11 p.m. He asked Whinfield if he could lend him any money, to which Whinfield replied that he had nothing to lend because he was unemployed. At that, Smithies walked over to the kitchen sink, picked up the hatchet, walked back to the sofa where William Whinfield sat and, without speaking a word, proceeded to beat him about the head. Calmly he then placed the hatchet on the kitchen table and told the two children that 'I meant to do that some time since.' Because he had not killed his defenceless co-lodger outright, police had arrested him for unlawful wounding. But since the coroner's jury returned a verdict of wilful killing, Smithies was rearrested after the hearing and formally charged with murder.

Viewing a body in Victorian times.

1887 Tragedy ruined Doncaster Cup Day. As crowds gathered around the racecourse at Doncaster for the St Leger meeting, a train from Sheffield packed with racegoers stood beneath Hexthorpe bridge, about 1½ miles outside Doncaster, while tickets were being collected. Just as the guard began to signal that it was clear to move, the train was struck in the rear by the Manchester express. Its last two carriages were reduced to matchwood in a matter of seconds, scattering the dead and dying across both sides of the track. Hundreds lay where they had been thrown and efforts to transport the worst-injured went on throughout the day. As breakdown gangs began clearing up that evening, twenty bodies lay covered by blankets in a field beside Hexthorpe village.

16 September

1813 A nineteenth-century magic pill.

17 September

Dr Boerhaave's Infallible Red Pill.

Persons of either sex (assisted by the invaluable copious directions therewith given) are enabled to eradicate the most malignant VENEREAL INFECTION and to facilitate the recovery with ease and safety, certainty and secrecy in a few days.

For Bilious Diseases, Scurvy, Scrofula, Impurities of the blood, the efficacies of this medicine are so well known and highly attested for 50 years past, that any further comment is rendered unnecessary.

18 SEPTEMBER 1862 Brian Cohen committed suicide by cutting his throat after it was discovered that twenty-eight gold watches on sale at his jeweller's shop in Sheffield had been stolen over a period of weeks from various jewellers in Swansea.

19 SEPTEMBER 1842 Robert Crow (aged 25) and James Bates (aged 21) were indicted for committing highway robbery on the outskirts of Barnsley. They had attacked an elderly man, William Dyson, striking him over the head twice with a metal bar and then dragging him from his horse and stealing 18s from his pockets, together with a pair of spectacles and two memorandum books. They had been caught three days before the hearing and identified by Dyson. It was an open-and-shut case; the judge sentenced them to be transported for fifteen years.

20 SEPTEMBER 1932 John Ellis, Britain's executioner for twenty-three years, having been involved in 203 executions, including those of some of the most celebrated murderers in criminal history, and, of course, Emily Swan and John Gallagher, the Wombwell murderers, stood on his front doorstep at his Rochdale home and committed suicide with his cut-throat razor.

21 SEPTEMBER 1841 A report described the inquest held at the Courthouse, Rotherham, on the body of Hannah Crossland (aged 54). After a drunken argument with her husband Joshua, landlord of the Waggon and Horses public house at Masbrough, over his decision to paint the pub windows shut, he had thrown the paintbrush at her in a fit of temper. Unintentionally the brush had hit her, handle first, on the forehead and caused a wound the size of a sixpenny piece that penetrated as far as her skull. Local surgeon Mr Wilkinson told the court he had bandaged the wound and told Hannah to remain quiet, indoors and away from all draughts. Ten days after the incident she had died as a result of her injury. Joshua denied ever having hurled the brush across the room and insisted she had simply fallen against a wall. The coroner refused to accept his version but, despite his serious reservations, told the jury that because no evidence existed to support either the wife's or the husband's story he could not be charged with any criminal offence. The extremely lucky publican walked free from the courtroom.

22 SEPTEMBER 1917 A shocking case of starvation was reported in the Yorkshire Times on this day. Harold Barrow, a collier working for the Yorkshire Main Colliery, and his wife Nellie both stood in the dock at Doncaster accused of allowing their newly born baby to die of starvation. For the first four weeks of its life milk had been delivered to the house to provide the necessary nourishment. Harold Barrow decided a month was long enough and so cancelled the supply and spent the money on other foodstuffs, none of which the baby could eat. Two days later it was dead. Both denied their culpability, arguing that the reason the milk was stopped was because the baby had stopped drinking it. The magistrate accused both of being callous in their

dealings with the baby but released Nellie because he believed she had been influenced by her husband. Harold was sent to prison for three months with hard labour.

1623 George Flower left his wife and two children at home and travelled to Wheatley to find work. Local landowner Mr Mountjoy set him to work on his farm and found lodgings for him with Widow Stubbs. But the good widow wanted more than a fair rent. Over the period of the summer she persuaded George to steal sixteen sheaves of barley, which she then stored inside her house. Unhappily for both of them the theft was quickly uncovered and good old George earmarked as the thief. He went to ground – literally – hiding among the hay, and Widow Stubbs began smuggling food out to him. As was bound to happen she was eventually seen and Mr Mountjoy had her arrested and imprisoned in Doncaster. George took a little longer to find. The villagers waited for him to attempt an escape, which he did once his food supply had run out, and after a brief chase they caught him near the river. In the fight that followed he was all but drowned before help arrived. George joined the good widow in prison for his part in the theft.
23 SEPTEMBER

1917 Zeppelin attacks on South Yorkshire were reported in the Yorkshire Times. After crossing the coast between midnight and 3 a.m. the airship bombed the mining and industrial areas of South Yorkshire, dropping a significant number of bombs, though none hit their intended target.
24 SEPTEMBER

1777 John Moore, a labourer from Doncaster, was found guilty of stealing several parcels of cloth, commonly called Wildbore Tammies, with a value of 1s from innkeeper Thomas Hardisty. The court sentenced him to three years' hard labour working on the River Thames.
25 SEPTEMBER

1914 Mexborough mother Alice Smith (aged 22) was found guilty and sentenced to death for the dreadful murder of her baby of 2 years and nine months. The court heard how she had picked the child up in a fit of temper and strangled it to death. The sentence was later commuted to life.
26 SEPTEMBER

1582 Doncaster's first plague victim, Percival Harryson, died upon this day. Over the next twelve months a total of 908 people died of the disease – a third of the town's population – and all were buried behind the Corn Market.
27 SEPTEMBER

Old Yorkshire Beliefs, Omens and Sayings
To rock a cradle without the baby in it is to doom it to an early death. To protect the child at birth a knife should be placed on the doorstep, as no witch or evil spirit can cross iron or steel to do the infant harm.
28 SEPTEMBER

1775 Elizabeth Westerman, wife of blacksmith Henry, was found guilty of stealing one canvas purse, valued at 10d but containing a number of gold coins, belonging to Doncaster yeoman Robert Raven. The judge sentenced her to seven
29 SEPTEMBER

years' transportation to His Majesty's plantation in America. As war broke out the same year, perhaps she was lucky enough to join the victors and become an American citizen.

WEST RIDING OF YORKSHIRE CONSTABULARY.

Hostile Air Craft.

Precautions to be Observed in Case of Air Raids.

NOTICE IS HEREBY GIVEN that when information of the approach of enemy aircraft is reported at night, preliminary public warning will be given by gas pressure being reduced to a minimum, and the electric light current being reduced to the lowest point short of being cut off.

This warning, being a precautionary measure, should not unduly alarm the public ; when given the following instructions must be obeyed :—

1.—All electric and gas lights must be extinguished and the gas turned off at the meter.

2.—Lights must remain extinguished until daylight, or until notice is given that the danger is past.

  NOTE. — It is not necessary to remain in darkness : candles only may be used, but no lights must be visible from outside.

3.—All street lamps and external lights will be extinguished, and on no account will bull's-eye lanterns, electric torches or flash lights, bicycle lamps, etc., be permitted to be used. The striking of matches in the streets is also strictly prohibited.

4.—The gas must be turned off at the meter in lock-up shops and other like premises before being left for the night.

5.—Persons must not congregate in the streets, nor stand near windows, but seek cover.

6.—Outside doors should be closed, but not locked, and windows should be closed to prevent the admission of noxious gases.

7.— Bombs of any description must be left untouched, and information given to the police.

8.—Vehicular traffic will be held up, and no lights will be permitted, except in the case of tramcars unable to reach their Depôts. These will stand clear of cross roads, and expose a small red light in front and rear.

9.—The sounding of buzzers, hooters, bugles, and the ringing of bells, etc., is forbidden.

10.—Congregations in places of worship and audiences at places of entertainment should disperse and proceed home. Workpeople in munition factories, etc., are advised to take shelter until the danger is passed, when work may be resumed.

11.—Persons should not telephone to the police station unless on matters of great urgency. The police will do their best to circulate such information as may be considered necessary, and the public are warned against spreading alarming reports.

12.—All instructions given by the military, and the police (regular and special) must be immediately obeyed.

ARTHUR C. QUEST,
ACTING CHIEF CONSTABLE,
WEST RIDING OF YORKSHIRE.

County Chief Constable's Office,
Wakefield, 29th February, 1916.

PRINTED AT THE COUNTY CHIEF CONSTABLE'S OFFICE, WAKEFIELD.

Hostile aircraft poster, 1916. (Author's Collection)

1859 Murder in Laughton-Le-Morthen. John Taylor Whitworth had been courting young Sally Hare since the early days of her arrival at the Cuthberts' farm five months previously. Whitworth was a constant visitor to the farm and the Cuthberts had got used to his frequent appearances. When he arrived to help with the milking they saw little wrong with it and left the two of them before the kitchen fire at around 10 p.m. Here they stayed until a little after 1 a.m. when Sally, conscious of the late hour, told him it was time he left and, as she had done for months, put her bonnet on and set off to walk with him as far as the village. Whitworth, who harboured a belief that Sally had been unfaithful, waited until they were some distance from the house before he accused her of meeting another man. She denied it but an argument ensued, resulting in her running into the Cuthberts' bedroom minutes later, screaming that she had been murdered. Blood soaked the front of her dress from wounds to her fingers, chin and throat and there was nothing either of them could do to stem the flow.

Lying Sally on a bed in the next room they did their best to save her life but after a medical examination an hour or so later it became clear that nothing

Morthen village, *c.* 1900. *(Doncaster Archives)*

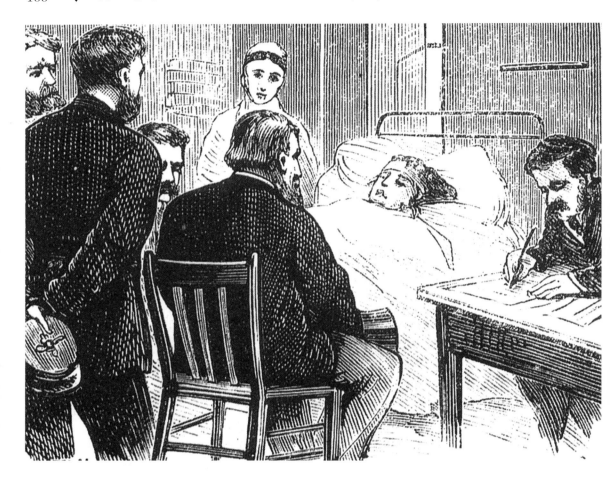

Taking a dying
deposition.
(Steve Jones, Wicked
Publications)

was going to save her. Police were sent for and a statement taken before
she finally expired. Whitworth, devastated by what had happened, walked
into a police station at Worksop just after dawn and gave his version of the
night's events to the duty officer. The two vastly contradictory accounts were
eventually placed before a jury. Sally's accused Whitworth of deliberately
stabbing her in a bizarre attempt at forcing her into a double suicide pact.
Whitworth insisted it had been Sally who had attacked him and seized his
knife in an attempt to kill him; her killing had been purely accidental. At
his trial in December 1859 the jury accepted the deceased's version and
Whitworth was executed for murder in January 1860.

OCTOBER

Police officers at Rotherham, 1925.
(Rotherham Archives and Local Studies)

1 OCTOBER **1897** James Naylor, a boot-riveter of Barnsley, was fined 10s at the court-house after being convicted of setting a ferret down a rabbit hole. In his defence he argued that he had done no such thing but had simply lost the ferret in woodland and had been forced to dig it out. The rabbit found dead had obviously been an accident.

2 OCTOBER **1888** A report appeared concerning the case of Doctor William Henry Burke who murdered his 9-year-old daughter, Aileen. The Burke family had lived at the Manor House at Monk Bretton and were a well regarded and highly thought of family. As surgeon to Monk Bretton, Carlton Main Colliery and Monckton Main, Dr Burke moved among Barnsley's well-heeled classes and earned significantly from the association. He was also partial to a drink. After taking his wife and daughter into the best room of the Normanton Arms, where they stayed until 11 p.m., he had calmly pulled a gun from his pocket and with deliberate aim shot the little girl dead. He then turned the weapon upon himself and fired one more shot. He was out of luck: the bullet did not kill him, but entered his chest.

The whole event was watched by the best witness a courtroom could ever have: local beat bobby PC Francis Emslie. He had entered the pub to check that the landlord was closing for the night and as he opened the door into the best room he clearly saw the whole awful event unravel. Helpless to stop the killing, all he was able to do was tend the wounded father. Burke had sustained severe injuries from his attempt at suicide and for some time it was touch and go whether he would live. For almost three months he was forced to lie in a hospital bed, where despite questioning he showed no contrition. In court he claimed that the whole event was an accident, that the gun had fired unintentionally. A letter found at the scene and in the doctor's handwriting seemed to indicate that he had been having an affair with another woman and that suicide had always been his intention. There was no mention though of little Aileen. Burke's submission was accordingly dismissed by the court and he was sentenced to death. The sentence was later commuted to life, but Burke did not survive long after that because of his self-inflicted bullet wound.

Doncaster Guild Hall. (*Doncaster Archives*)

3 OCTOBER **1894** Doncaster's Lord Mayor, Henry Woodmansey, died upon this day after slipping on a flower. After attending a party given by some young ladies, their husbands and

friends who had assisted in setting up and running a bazaar to raise funds for the Infirmary, he had made his apologies and left to go to his bed at around 2 a.m. As he descended the stone staircase he trod on a flower that had fallen from someone's lapel earlier in the evening and fell headlong down the stone steps. Carried to his rooms with a severe scalp wound which bled profusely, the ill-starred Mayor never regained consciousness.

1867 Prostitute Annie Edwards was found lying on the floor in the front room of her house, suffering from severe head wounds. Still conscious, she identified her attacker as William Harrison who, she claimed, had kicked her violently during an unprovoked attack. Police found him cowering under her bed upstairs and arrested him for assault. But Annie had been mortally wounded and died later that day. William was eventually charged with her manslaughter and sent for trial at Leeds.

4 OCTOBER

Crowd gathering outside Annie Edwards' house.
(Steve Jones, Wicked Publications)

5 OCTOBER **1897** Before magistrates on a charge of jumping on a paramour, Alfred Hayes, a miner from Barnsley, was sent to prison for three months' hard labour. The court was told that on a night out to the Butchers' Arms in September he had dragged his victim from the bar by her hair, thrown her to the floor then stamped on her face – all because another man had bought her a whisky. Sadly, she refused to testify against him, or the distasteful creature would have been shut away for a good deal longer.

6 OCTOBER **1856** Thomas Askern (aged 33) of Maltby, Rotherham, was announced as one of York's new public executioners and later carried out his first execution, of a Leeds man named William Dove, in front of a large crowd assembled outside the castle. Reportedly paid 10s for each execution he was kept busy for much of his life, still doing the job in 1874, which is the date of the last available record.

7 OCTOBER **1840** An inquest was held at the Horse and Jockey Inn on Ward Green on the body of George Blackburn, farmer, who had been beaten to death outside his home after spending the day travelling round his customers in Barnsley, collecting debts. John Mitchell, alias 'Gypsy Jack Mitchell', had been clearly identified as being among a group of four men who had lain in wait for the farmer, and had been arrested within hours. Three other arrests quickly followed but the court was told that only Gypsy Jack's clothing exhibited blood staining. He denied any involvement, but after the coroner's verdict of wilful murder he stood trial later in the year and was sentenced to hang. Following a confession hours before his execution, the sentence was commuted to one of transportation. A poem read in the pubs of South Yorkshire proclaimed his fate.

> Near Vernon's Mount is the blood stained land,
> Where Blackburn fell to the ruffians' hand,
> The place is known as the Elmhurst farm,
> 'Twas there he dwelt with no thought of harm,
> But he was waylaid near his own door stone,
> And with fatal stroke he was made to moan.
>
> A stone was hurled with a fearful bound,
> Which laid him low on the damp cold ground,
> His servant screamed for she saw him fall,
> The wretches fled o'er the planting wall,
> From the barracks near sped some soldiers brave,
> But they were too tardy his life to save.
>
> Stern justice reached the worst of the gang,
> His brow was seared with foul murder's brand,
> And he was sent to a penal land,
> Like a beast of prey to be barred and chained,
> In thrall to be held while his life remained.

MURDER OF A GAMEKEEPER.

NEAR ROTHERHAM.

APPREHENSION OF THE SUPPOSED MURDERERS.

CONFESSIONS OF TWO ACCOMPLICES.

"Murder will out." So runs the old adage, and such is likely conclusively to prove the case with regard to the murder of William Lilley, the gamekeeper, at Silverwood near Ravenfield, a week or two ago. During the present week a number of men have been apprehended by the police and charged with being concerned in the fatal encounter. As our readers are aware, directly after the murder the police instituted inquiries, and in addition to the staff of the Rotherham police force, under the charge of Mr Superintendent Gillett, the Chief Constable of the Riding sent down Mr Detective Officer Hockaday from Wakefield, who has since acted in conjunction with the former. Although we believe a number of persons well known to several of the Rotherham police officers were at once marked out as being exceedingly likely to have had some share in the perpetration of the hideous deed, the utmost difficulty was experienced for some time in getting any tangible clue, or at all events, in deducing any conclusive evidence such as would warrant their apprehension. The officers, however pursued their investigations with the utmost assiduity, and with not a little skill. Many circumstances combined to render the task a most difficult one. The keepers who were out with Lilley on the night of the murder have shewed considerable reluctance to give any very valuable information as to the parties engaged in the encounter, if indeed they were possessed of any of such information. At the coroner's inquest this was especially noticeable, and in one or two instances, the reticence or backwardness of the witnesses called forth the rebuke of the coroner. To the details of the evidence of the three keepers we need not now refer, as the whole will be sufficiently fresh in the minds of our readers. The poachers themselves left nothing on the scene of the fatal encounter which might have served to lead to their identity, and their clothes, it may be anticipated, were not marked with the blood of their victim, as no very close struggle could have taken place. The only weapons necessary to produce death may very possibly have been found in the field, and none others were left behind. It may not unreasonably have been supposed then by some that, taking all the circumstances into consideration, there was at least a great probability of the murderers for some time evading the iron grasp of the law. There was hope, however, in the very fact that there were several men engaged, and also that a golden bribe of £350 would at least offer some inducement to any of those whose necks were less in danger than were those who really struck the fatal blows to inform. The officers in the course of their enquiries met with considerable valuable circumstantial evidence which when carefully reviewed tended fully to strengthen their previous convictions as to who were the guilty parties. It may be here mentioned that immediately after the murder several of the supposed guilty persons were detained and examined by the police. They were also confronted by the keepers, who could not, however, speak to any of them, having been of the poaching party. The suspected ones were all of them known as notorious poachers, and some of the officers of the Rotherham police, to whom much credit is due for their sagacity, have for some time kept a very watchful eye upon them. After they were set at liberty they did not loose sight of them. Every article of evidence had been carefully collected, and the officers have pursued their investigations to the utmost extent in their power. At length when the matter was considered in a sufficiently ripe state to bring it boldly to an issue, Mr Gillett, in conjunction with Mr Hockaday, applied on Monday last to the Rotherham bench of magistrates for warrants to be issued for the apprehension of fourteen men. The application was not an ordinary one, but if we are rightly informed, the superintendent of police at Rotherham laid before the Bench sufficient information to induce instant compliance with the request. Accordingly, an efficient staff of police under the direction of Mr Superintendent Gillett. assembled at a late hour on

1910 Annie Cauldwell (29) murdered her 1-month-old baby son, Bruce, by drowning him in a bath of water because she '. . . wanted the little lamb to go to heaven'. According to her husband Frank, a colliery labourer, she had shown no violent traits during her pregnancy and he thought the child safe in her care. But the local Anston doctor disagreed: he told the inquest that he had been forced to commit Annie to a mental asylum some years earlier and that her mental state had always been suspect. Charged with wilful murder, she stood trial two months later and was declared insane.

8 OCTOBER

1852 William Kay of Barnsley was robbed of 15s just after midnight by three unidentified robbers who had lain in wait as he walked along the Pontefract road. Despite extensive searches and wanted posters, no one was ever charged.

9 OCTOBER

1865 At about 10 p.m. this night Bramley gamekeeper William Lilley charged across an open field at Silverwood, intent on arresting a group of poachers as they set their nets. Well armed and accompanied by two other keepers, he believed the men in front of him would either scatter or else give themselves up. He was wrong. The other keepers, who had failed to help co-ordinate the attack, did not charge with him and therefore when he met the poaching group he was alone. The first man he met struck him a single blow to the head that forced him to his knees. Others quickly joined in and within a few short minutes they had beaten him to death. The other keepers never managed to get within striking distance of Lilley's attackers: pinned down by a lethal hail of bricks and stones hurled by the other poachers, some dozen men, they were forced to flee from the field.

10 OCTOBER

Newspaper article reporting the murder of William Lilley. (*Rotherham Advertiser*)

Lilley's body was discovered by Police Constable Jabes Fowler some two hours after the murderous assault. It lay where the gamekeeper had sustained the first blow, beside a blood-covered hedge stake believed to have been one of the murder weapons. The policeman arranged for the body to be transported back to Lilley's home in Bramley. Eight men were subsequently arrested and charged with the attack. One of the eight became an approver (turned Queen's evidence), which was the breakthrough police had been looking for. It was he who named the key attackers: John Teale, William Sykes, Henry Bone and John Bentcliffe. All were found guilty but the jury ignored the judge's direction and refused to return a murder verdict. In its place they recorded one of manslaughter. Despite this, the judge then ordered they be transported to the penal colony in Western Australia for up to twenty years. Their notoriety was recorded in verse form by the *Rotherham Advertiser*.

At Wickersley there lived a gamekeeper,
Of honour and great fame,
He took delight in the dead of night,
Preserving of his game.

On the tenth night of October he left his wife and children,
The weather was cold and chilly;
The poachers shed the blood near Silverwood
Of famous William Lilley.

It was Sykes, Teale, and Bone, fought with hedgestakes, sticks and stones,
More like savages in a mêlée;
They shed the blood near Silverwood
Of famous William Lilley.

The murderers found no resting-place,
Wherever they did scout;
And Hockaday from Wakefield came,
And searched the villains out.

The crime of murder will stick close to them,
Wherever they may be,
And stain the spot they finish at last –
If on the gallows tree.

Though years and centuries may pass away,
Then human blood will chill
To hear the tale of wilful murder
Of poor William of the hill.

Poor Lilley is gone, and we greet him,
Though in these woods we will meet no more;
Still we hope some day to meet him
On some peaceful, happy shore.

A whipping 'at the cart's tail'.
(The Johnson Collection)

1637   At Doncaster today John Walker, a labourer of Ecclesfield, pleaded not guilty to a charge of grand larceny after being accused of stealing a Bible worth 5s. As thefts of more than a shilling brought the death penalty if proven, he pleaded not guilty. The jury disagreed but reduced the charge to one of petty larceny. The judge ordered that Walker be whipped: painful but not as painful as hanging.

1858   On this day Isaac Wood (19) was fatally shot in front of witnesses outside the Rock Inn, Hoyland. Wood had been gambling for beer throughout the afternoon with William Hague, until the two men had a falling out. After the quarrelling pair had been separated by other patrons of the pub, Hague ran home, saying he 'would fetch something that would do him'. He returned minutes later with a shotgun. Realising what was about to happen, a bystander called Edwards tried to wrestle him to the ground and seize the gun but he was beaten away. Hague then aimed and fired once. The shot hit Isaac in the left arm, smashing his elbow, wounding the left side of his face and mouth, and shattering a tooth, and spread across the left side of his chest. Fully conscious, he made a statement to police but died the following day after undergoing surgery to remove his left arm. William Hague was committed on a coroner's warrant to the Winter Assizes.

13 October **1737** Mary Stanfield, a Doncaster spinster, was found guilty of stealing one silver spoon, a hat, a scarlet cloak, two shifts, one gown, a child's frock, two children's cloaks, a pair of leather clogs, a pair of stockings, one cambric handkerchief, one hood, one comb, a razor and a pot of butter, all the property of Mr Edward Green, gentleman. She was sentenced to be whipped.

14 October **1866** A reward of £1,100 was offered after the house of Thomas Fearney-hough had been blown apart by gunpowder a week earlier. He naturally wanted to apprehend the culprit, but a reward of such huge proportions for a crime that – despite its intent – had caused no casualties was most unusual. Perhaps it was so unusual as to be thought unbelievable, which could be why no one ever stepped forward to name the person who had stuffed the explosive into a tin and carefully placed it in the centre of Fearneyhough's cellar.

15 October **1896** At midnight West Riding Constabulary handed over the policing of Barnsley to Barnsley Borough Police after being in charge since 1 January 1857. It made little initial impact on the force but led to more efficient working practices in the long term.

16 October **1867** Today saw two horrific deaths in a fireworks explosion. Keen to celebrate Bonfire Night a Mr Copley had stored his fireworks in what he believed to be the safest place in Sheffield, a back room above his hairdressing shop on Campo Lane. None of his customers were aware as they sat in the barber's chair that above their heads sat a time bomb waiting to explode, which is exactly what happened when the fireworks were inadvertently caught by a spark. Edwin Allnut and William Simpson, on their monthly visit for a trim, were killed as the shop went up in flames.

17 October **1868** After a row over company finances between the two partners of Slater, Brunt Co., a steelworks on Shoreham Street, Sheffield, Slater, in a fit of anger, took a pistol from his desk and shot George Brunt in the face. Luckily for the wounded man his injuries were not life-threatening but perhaps Slater did not realise that. Arrested by police and charged with attempted murder, he was sent to Wakefield prison to await trial. Desperate not to be brought to court, he had other ideas and as he was being taken up a stone staircase, he jumped over the balustrade to his death.

18 October **1841** The death was reported of Joseph Gales in Raleigh, North Carolina, at the age of 80. A native of Sheffield, he had become notorious in June of 1794 when, as the owner and editor of the *Sheffield Register* newspaper, he had fled the country after officers had been sent to his Sheffield home to arrest him for unspecified crimes. Not prepared to take his chances under the English legal system, he hid among friends in the city for months, and later across Yorkshire, until he could catch a boat to France. After spending some time on the Continent he managed to pay his way to America. From Philadelphia he began to publish the *Independent Gazetteer* then travelled across country to North Carolina, where he became owner of the Raleigh Register, which he published for forty years.

1840 Doncaster Watch Committee minutes record the dismissal of day watchman Thomas Platts. A number of complaints had been lodged against him by members of the public over the way they had been dealt with and his attitude towards them. The police management decided that since he had been suspended for four weeks in 1836 for similar offences, his services would no longer be required. He was accordingly fired.

19 OCTOBER

Old Yorkshire Beliefs, Omens and Sayings

A child baptised must not have font water wiped from the face, but allow it to dry naturally. The christening cap must also be left on the baby's head for twelve weeks. But never be the first to be baptised in a new church, as the child will be claimed by the devil.

20 OCTOBER

1913 The case was reported on this day of domestic servant Alice Sagar who was sentenced by a Doncaster court to five years' imprisonment. She had apparently developed a skill in house robbery that was most unusual. Applying for domestic jobs she would attend interviews, then if opportunity allowed would try to stay in the house after the interview had ended. From her hiding place she would watch as the house settled down for the night and wait patiently until everyone had retired to bed. At that point she would come out from her secret place and systematically move through as many rooms as she could safely manage without awakening anyone, stealing as much as she could easily carry away. Unfortunately at a house at Balby after following her usual pattern, whether by accident or intent, she set the place on fire as she left. Roused by the sudden smoke, the couple in the upstairs bedroom saw her from the window and she was quickly caught by police. She offered no explanation for the fire but acknowledged her talent as a thief.

21 OCTOBER

1856 The funeral took place on this day of John Whitaker, a Thrybergh farmer, who had been brutally murdered and robbed on the road outside Dalton five days earlier. A rich man but one who had lived frugally since inheriting his father's farm, he had been returning from a market in York and was carrying over £200. Conscious of the dangers of attempting to walk home at night he sought lodgings in Rotherham but was unsuccessful, and so travelled to Dalton Brook in the company of another man who was taking sheep to Bramley. He had intended to try to get a room at the Grapes Hotel but

22 OCTOBER

The windmill where John Whitaker sought refuge. *(Rotherham Archives and Local Studies)*

by the time he arrived it had shut up for the night. There was little choice but to keep going and after parting company with his fellow traveller he set out on the last leg of his journey. At the bottom of Winney Hill, near the Grapes Hotel, he was surrounded by a group of men who attacked him, beat him with leather coshes, robbed him of his £200 and left him for dead on the roadside.

After lying unconscious for an hour or so he recovered his senses enough to stagger to a nearby windmill. He knocked on the door and received some rudimentary medical attention from the owner, but stubbornly refused a bed, insisting on completing his journey home. The owner's nephew walked with him for the last few miles to his farmhouse but by the time the two men arrived Whitaker was in a dreadful state and bleeding badly. A doctor was sent for and the wounds dressed but the farmer lost consciousness during the night and died the next morning from complications caused by a fractured skull.

No one was ever caught for the crime but in May of 1882, some twenty-six years later, a certain Aaron Leedham, arrested after a fight with his wife, was accused by her of being among the men who had carried out the robbery and murder. Leedham would have been only 16 at the time – a point not lost on the police – but after a visit from his wife he made a statement to the effect that he had acted as lookout for his father and two other men on the night Whitaker had been attacked. Furthermore, he told police that as well as money, they had stolen a watch, and that watch was still in circulation. The father was dead by this time, but one of the other two men he named was arrested in Sheffield. However, because of the lack of corroborative evidence the case never came to trial and the watch was never recovered.

John Whitaker's gravestone in Thrybergh churchyard.

1760 James Cowood, a private in the West Riding Militia, stood before magistrates charged with endeavouring, by force of arms, to raise a mutiny among the men with whom he served and, further, with escaping from Doncaster prison after his arrest. He pleaded guilty but the records do not show the sentence passed.

23 OCTOBER

1842 *A pocket full of pigeons.* George Hibberd, George Birkhead and Henry Cutt appeared before magistrates, charged with stealing pigeons from a Mr Luke White at Bolton upon Dearne. Several days after the theft, police, responding to a tip-off, had lain in wait one night until dawn, hidden in bushes along Brightside Lane, Sheffield. They had been told that the thieves intended to fly the pigeons in a race in the morning. Police patience was rewarded when all three turned up, and they sprang the trap. After a serious scuffle Sheffield constable John Newman managed to disarm Birkhead, known to have been the ringleader, and twenty pigeons were removed from each man's jacket pockets. While the gang were in custody it was discovered that they had stolen pigeons from all over Rotherham and that it was Hibberd, not Birkhead, who was the instigator and ringleader with a criminal record stretching back to 1828. He was therefore transported for seven years on the grounds that his continued presence was of no use to the country.

24 OCTOBER

A policeman, *c.* 1890.

1862 An inquest at the Red Lion Inn, Mexborough, on the body of Fanny Chapman (aged 52) heard how being restrained by her husband had led to her death. Known locally as a fiery woman with a mean temperament, she had threatened friends and neighbours alike. After arriving home in a state of intoxication she lost her temper when her husband demanded food and, grabbing the poker from the fireside, set about beating him into submission. Husband Christian, a tailor by trade and generally a mild-mannered man, grappled with her around the room finally managing to pin her down across the back of a chair, holding the hand wielding the poker at a good arm's length. At that juncture neighbours ran into the house and managed to separate the couple. All was well for the next two weeks though she complained of pains in her left side. These grew progressively worse until her breathing had become extremely laboured and she died. Police blamed the husband for the death and looked to the coroner to support their view; but he chose to return a verdict of accidental death. Christian Chapman had been lucky indeed.

25 OCTOBER

26 OCTOBER

1839   An inquest opened on this day at Sheffield's coroner's office into the death of a baby discovered murdered in Burngreave Wood. The child, weighing 5¾lb, was 20in long, and its face had been disfigured on the right side as a result of being either beaten or thrown against something hard. According to local surgeon Mr Chesman none of the injuries could have been accidental. In the dock Sarah Auty (aged 35), believed to be the child's mother, remained impassive even though she knew the court believed her responsible for the killing. She refuted all evidence that she had been pregnant or had lately given birth to the dead child. But the good doctor disagreed: he told the coroner that there could be no doubt that the woman had recently given birth and that the delivery of that disputed birth must have been within the previous ten days.

Sarah's life had been one of severe hardship.

Sarah's father, Joseph Auty, did his daughter no favours when it came to speculation about the baby's antecedents. He told the court, possibly in all innocence, that his daughter often slept in the same bed as himself and his son. Gasps around the room brought a serious admonishment from the coroner regarding such incestuous behaviour. But he failed to see the connection. Witnesses filed into the room all pointing the finger of suspicion and confirming the doctor's diagnosis that Sarah had been pregnant. The verdict upheld the police view that the baby had definitely been murdered, but the coroner, despite all the circumstantial evidence to the contrary, refused to offer up a warrant of murder against the young woman.

27 OCTOBER

1846   Appearing before the bench on this day was Sarah Ann Hague for inciting her friend, Ann Stothard, to steal money from Sarah's father. She and her father had been involved in numerous rows over the years; Sarah had also stolen from him before but had never been brought before the courts for doing it. This time, possibly because the father did not realise at the time the theft was carried out that it had been set up by his own daughter, the police had been called to investigate. It mattered little to the court, which sentenced Sarah to four months in prison.

28 OCTOBER

1862   Thomas Slater found himself in a Sheffield courtroom after murdering his own mother for the price of a new pair of clogs. His old ones were worn out and he needed money to buy another pair; that money could only come from his mother, because he had no means of support. She refused, and in the fierce argument that ensued she tried to hit him across the head with a poker. But being younger and more agile he struck her a telling blow with his fist, hitting her squarely in the mouth. Her lips turned black and she died hours later. The magistrates referred the case to the Assize Court. Here the murder charge was lifted after the judge accepted his petition that he had been under severe provocation when he struck the fatal blow. The charge was lessened to manslaughter.

1648 Colonel Thomas Rainsborough was murdered on this day outside his lodgings at the market end of Baxtergate in Doncaster. One of Cromwell's most valued colonels and a genius at siege warfare, he had been sent north from London to take charge of the siege of Pontefract Castle, where remnants of the Royalist army were causing severe problems throughout South Yorkshire. A man of huge renown, having fought at Naseby and Bristol in the first Civil War and having assisted in quelling the Kent rebellion earlier in the year, he had gained a fearful reputation after capturing Colchester at the end of the summer. Yet his arrival at Pontefract had met with disdain from Sir Hugh Cholmely who considered the Colonel to be his social inferior, no more than a 'bare Colonel of Foot', and refused to hand over his command. Rainsborough took lodgings in Doncaster until the matter could be resolved.

But while Cholmely held little regard for the Colonel's reputation the same could not be said for those trapped inside the castle. They feared the man who had executed Colchester's commanders and they set in motion a plot to capture him and hold him for ransom. William Paulden was given the task of breaking out from the castle and effecting the capture. With twenty-two horsemen he rode first

29 OCTOBER

A cavalier of Charles I's defeated army.

to Mexborough so that they could approach Doncaster along the banks of the River Don. The band paused near Conisbrough while they sent a spy to reconnoitre the town, then entered through St Sepulchre Gate claiming they had travelled from Rotherham with urgent letters from Oliver Cromwell. Once in the town they found Rainsborough and, during a struggle to take him prisoner, killed him.

30 OCTOBER   **1842**   Charles Rhodes (aged 24) and Thomas Leatham (aged 25) were sentenced to death after being found guilty of carrying out a burglary at Barnsley. It was not their first offence and the two were known for handling stolen goods. Sentence was later commuted to transportation for life.

31 OCTOBER   **1888**   The *Barnsley Chronicle* reported on the health of Police Constable Tomlin, who had been cruelly attacked in September and stabbed several times in his right thigh. It was doubtful that he would be able to resume his duties because of the amount of damage the knife had done. Ben Armitage, a local man, had already been arrested and charged with attempted murder after the constable had been able to give details of the unprovoked attack near Victoria Bridge.

NOVEMBER

London police sent to assist in dealing with industrial unrest in Sheffield, 1896.
(Sheffield Libraries, Archives and Local Studies)

1 November   **1833**   Six convicts escaped from Sheffield's Town Hall after all had been found guilty of crimes ranging from theft to manslaughter and all sentenced to be transported to Australia. A cell had been left unlocked and none of the prisoners needed a second invitation.

2 November   **1841**   An inquest was held on the body of tragic Ann Fellows who had starved to death in her Sheffield home. Ann's first husband had been sentenced to death for robbery and her second had died, leaving her and her two children to survive on parish handouts. She had been unable to feed herself properly on the 3s that she received each week, and had died after being refused admittance to Ecclesfield workhouse on the grounds that she was young enough to fend for herself. Harsh times indeed!

3 November   **1842**   Habitual burglar William Woodhead stood before a court charged with breaking into a Sheffield shop and stealing a number of men's boots. Most of the ill-gotten gains he had promptly sold on to local men, all of whom were quick to identify him once police enquiries began. Also found in his bedroom were ladies' gowns from a variety of shops, which he had not yet managed to dispose of. At his trial the judge initially sentenced him to seven years' transportation; however, Woodhead was brought back to the dock after the judge consulted his law books and realised that the transportation penalty for breaking and entering had to be ten to fifteen years. He therefore amended his earlier sentence and banished the thief across the seas for ten years.

4 November   **1720**   Mary Jane Bligh, widow, was found guilty at Doncaster of stealing a pair of silver spoons and a shirt. Whether she had ever stolen goods before is not recorded but the sentence was certainly severe. Magistrates sentenced her to be whipped.

5 November   **1863**   Police Constables Swift and Howlden of Sheffield police were viciously attacked on the road between Darnall and Attercliffe after disturbing two pigeon-stealers. Both culprits were armed and in the fight that followed their discovery, the two policemen were badly injured, allowing their intended quarry to make good their escape. Happily for the constables they survived; what's more they had recognised their attackers. James and George Law were known offenders and police began to scour the country for them. The fugitives were eventually tracked down to Birmingham. At their subsequent trial James, the greater felon, received a ten-year sentence, while his brother was handed four years.

6 November   **1862**   James Whiteley (aged 36), a serial forger, was found guilty of uttering a counterfeit half-crown at Sheffield and, having already been convicted of a series of similar crimes, was sent to prison for four years' penal servitude.

7 November   **1852**   A missed footing brought death in Wombwell Woods. John White (aged 33), landlord of the Elephant Inn, Tingle Bridge, went walking through the woods with two friends, fellow landlord John Hall and Lord Fitzwilliam's bookkeeper, William Cooper. A keen huntsman, he had taken his shotgun on the chance that there would be game to shoot. At a little after 4 p.m. as the light began to fade, the three decided to make their way back home before darkness set in. As they emerged from the woodland interior into open land John White stumbled and the gun went off. Shot ripped a hole in his side and despite the best efforts of his friends he died within minutes.

A late nineteenth-century huntsman.

1858 Strike-breakers George Naylor and his friend Bentley were attacked as they left Warren Vale pit, Rawmarsh. The two had agreed to work despite the pit workforce of 1,200 men having been sacked and served with eviction notices because they had gone on strike. At the end of this, their first day at work, they found their new neighbours waiting for them as they left the colliery. Initially a crowd of some sixty boys gathered around them, hurling stones at the men's backs and calling them 'black sheep'. But this small assembly began to swell as they made their way out of Warren Vale and by the time they reached Rose Hill and Naylor's house the numbers had grown to over 2,000. Police, heavily outnumbered, forced a path to the door but were then trapped inside with the two miners as the crowd, by now a raging mob, hurled bricks and stones at anything that moved. Someone fired a gun. Sheltering on the floor the occupants of the house managed to avoid being hit but not a window survived and there they had to stay until police reinforcements arrived to scatter the crowd.

8 NOVEMBER

1821 In a late sitting of Sheffield's magistrates' court a tramp – an old sailor, complete with huge bushy beard – was brought before the bench for vagrancy and begging. But this was begging with a difference: in order to excite sympathy the man had deliberately created a distressing wound on one of his arms, which he would dutifully expose to any member of the public who passed by his makeshift bed on Westbar. The showing of the wound, made worse on a daily basis, created a lucrative fount of compassion that easily translated itself into money. Although the court initially believed that he was

9 NOVEMBER

merely a travelling act, moving from town to town in order to beg a living, it later transpired that he had a wife and child, and had travelled to Sheffield from Hull, en route to Liverpool, when he was arrested. The old salt was sent down for one month.

10 NOVEMBER 1842 A most unusual burglary was reported by the *Sheffield and Rotherham Independent* newspaper after Thomas Thornhill (aged 21), Joseph Hardy (aged 25) and Andrew Ward (aged 26) appeared in court charged with stealing ten hams, two sides of bacon, a crop of pork, a quantity of Boulogne sausages and assorted pies. Butcher George Hiller, whose shop fronted the street at Barkers Pool, did not witness the theft but realised quickly enough that his stock had been decimated. In an attempt to find the thieves he alerted the night watchman, who almost immediately stumbled upon three young men making their way down a side street. He shadowed them and, seeing them enter a house, went in after them. The watchman found the three sitting in front of a fire and as he asked them to stand up, a quantity of sausages and hams fell on to the floor. After a brief scuffle – involving a leg of pork as a weapon – the thieves were arrested and at their eventual trial sentenced to be transported for fifteen years.

11 NOVEMBER 1865 A report told of an impudent robbery at a Rotherham fishmonger's. An audacious passer-by managed to put out the gaslight inside the window of the shop and steal all the smoked haddock.

12 NOVEMBER 1825 A dead baby was reported to have been unearthed in a garden at Doncaster. Subsequent investigations showed that the child, a little girl, had been born alive to a local woman, Sarah Shaw. Cause of death had not been established but a number of witnesses had come forward to state that Sarah had certainly been pregnant and that since the birth no baby had been seen. She initially denied that the child was hers but was forced to retract her denials after a medical examination. Murder was the con-clusion of the coroner's court, based on evidence given by the examining surgeon, who told the court that in his opinion the child had lived. Sarah was duly arrested, charged with wilful murder and sent to York to await trial.

13 NOVEMBER 1841 A strange case came before Sheffield magistrates. The *Sheffield Mercury* reported that a number of barbers had appeared in court on this day for shaving their customers on a Sunday. Magistrates decided, after lengthy deliberation, that the observance of the Lord's Day, though paramount, would still be assured if all barbers stopped shaving at 9 a.m. They agreed that it was 'a work of necessity before nine o'clock, but not after-wards'. The case was dismissed.

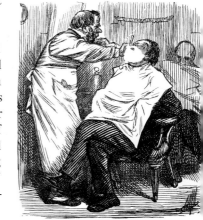

A Sheffield barber at work.

1897 A report emerged of a truly despicable murder at Barnsley. John Haliday, a pit sinker, had been living with Mary Ellen Dobson (aged 28) for a number of years. It was not a successful relationship and the two had parted on a number of occasions over the previous years. Haliday was a violent and nasty little man who often used his fists before using his brain. After yet another reconciliation neighbours heard shouts and screams from the house the couple shared. The nearest neighbour in the yard went outside and peered in through the kitchen window. Mary was lying on a bed and as the neighbour watched she clearly saw Haliday walk across the room and aim several kicks at her head. The house fell silent at that point and poor Mary, having been kicked so violently by a man wearing steel toecaps, died of her injuries. Haliday was arrested on a charge of wilful murder and Barnsley magistrates ordered him to stand trial for murder.

14 NOVEMBER

1904 An account of a savage killing was laid before the public. William Trubshaw, a glassworker from Barnsley, without any apparent provocation, murdered his wife and two children at their Mexborough home after a row and then committed suicide.

15 NOVEMBER

1908 Harold Booth stood before a court in Doncaster charged with setting fire to the Don Saw Mills in Conisbrough village. The mills, owned by his father, suffered over £1,000 of damage and Booth pleaded guilty to causing it. Angry after his father had threatened to evict him from the family home if he did not curb his drinking, the young man had stormed off to the Castle

16 NOVEMBER

Doncaster Road, Conisbrough, *c.* 1900. *(Doncaster Library and Information Services)*

Inn. Here he spent some time drowning his sorrows and while drunk decided that, as an act of pure malice, he would start the fire to spite his father. He was committed to trial at the Assizes and offered bail of £50, which he refused.

17 NOVEMBER   **1841**   William Stringer (aged 25) made a dying deposition to local police after being attacked and stabbed three times by his one-time friend and landlord, Henry Rodgers. Both men lived in Sheffield's Pinfold Street in what the *Sheffield and Rotherham Independent* described as housing fit only for the lowest characters. Stringer was a known thief, a man who had lived much of his life on the wrong side of the law but who nevertheless hated living in abject squalor. He had left Rodgers's lodgings because he found them to be filthy and he said so. That had led to friction with Rodgers and more so with Rodgers's wife, Elizabeth. She it was who precipitated his killing after physically attacking him as he stood in the street. Using her fists she hit him two or three times across the face, calling him a thief as she did so and daring him to strike her back.

Stringer needed no second invitation and with one blow put her on her back, abusing her verbally as she lay on the ground. In return she swore roundly at him and ran back to her house to fetch Henry Rodgers. Angered at his wife's mistreatment Rodgers snatched a shoemaker's knife from the table, ran out of the house and straight across the street to where Stringer stood. Without stopping to exchange any words he then stabbed his erstwhile friend three times: once in his side – the knife penetrating as far as the abdomen – and twice in the neck – once each side. There was never any chance that Stringer would survive. Treated by Charles Turton, who told him from the outset that he would not live through the night, he died in the early hours of the following morning. The inquest, held at the Town Hall, listened to all the evidence and issued a warrant for wilful murder against Henry Rodgers, ordering that he stand trial.

18 NOVEMBER   **1852**   James Ellis, John Green and Edward Marshall stood in the dock accused of passing forged notes through the Yorkshire Bank in Sheffield, Pontefract and Bradford. All were arrested with incriminating evidence about their persons and were easily pronounced guilty. Ellis, who had a long criminal record, was transported for life. The others were sent to prison for fifteen years each.

19 NOVEMBER   **1866**   After a falling-out of apprentices in a draper's shop on Sheffield's Fargate, Henry Gabites struck out at his fellow worker Arthur Allen with a hammer. Such was the violent force used that the young man was killed almost instantly. At his trial Gabites pleaded not guilty to murder but the jury threw out his plea and he was duly sentenced to death.

20 NOVEMBER   **1864**   Sheffield cutler James Wright was shot dead on this day by his good friend John Horsefield inside a public house at Wadsley. The gun was fired

accidentally but Horsefield was forced to endure the rigours of a murder trial in March of the following year.

1863 The death of Robert Hales, the Norfolk giant, took place at his public house, the Burgoyne Arms, on Langsett Road, Sheffield. He was 43 years old, measured 7ft 6in and weighed in at 452lb. 21 NOVEMBER

1835 The inquest into the death of John Hodgkinson of Sheffield returned a verdict that he had committed suicide in Eccleshall Woods by shooting himself while either temporarily insane or suffering from depression. 22 NOVEMBER

Old Yorkshire Beliefs, Omens and Sayings
Mourners should touch the body of the deceased while it lies in the coffin before burial to ensure good fortune for the living and allow the departed to go to his or her rest in peace. 23 NOVEMBER

1917 A nightmarish domestic accident took place in Hemsworth. It seemed like a normal Saturday morning for the Marsh family. Father, Peter Marsh, was upstairs lying on the bed trying to get their youngest to sleep, while his wife and three daughters were all downstairs in the kitchen. But in a departure from the usual Saturday morning routine his wife decided to leave their daughters alone for a few minutes while she walked down to the 24 NOVEMBER

Woodcut of a condemned man used in penny broadsheets in the early nineteenth century.

butcher's shop. It was to prove a tragic mistake. The eldest of the three girls, Louisa, suddenly began screaming and by the time her father managed to run downstairs she was aflame from head to foot, having been accidentally set alight by one of her younger sisters. Peter managed to dowse the flames but Louisa's burns were so extensive that she died shortly afterwards in the workhouse infirmary.

25 NOVEMBER   **1910**   In the dock on this day Mary Eleanor Richardson, wife of a Rotherham gardener, stood accused of the murder of her 3-week-old baby boy and the attempted murder of her 4-year-old son, Percy. According to witnesses she had appeared to be perfectly normal when, on a warm July day, they had seen her carrying the baby and walking hand-in-hand with the young boy through Parkgate. An hour later, however, things had changed. Another witness, who had been crossing a bridge over the River Don near where she had been seen earlier that day, told the court he had seen her standing in the water attempting to drown the 4-year-old. He ran to the water's edge and dragged both of them back to the bank, thus saving the boy's life – but too late to do anything for the baby. It was some time though before Mary told police that her baby had been drowned long before the passer-by intervened, and that she had allowed the body to float away. The judge, after listening to medical opinion, directed the jury to return a verdict of insanity.

26 NOVEMBER   **1867**   George Moverley stood in the dock at York accused of murdering his fellow worker William Burton. Both men worked at the Doncaster Plant Works

and knew each other well. Burton had tormented his attacker mercilessly over the preceding months and provoked a fight after an argument inside the works. In a fit of desperate anger Moverley grabbed at the first thing to come to hand and struck out. This was in fact a hammer; it is not known if Moverley was clear-headed enough to realise this, but what is certain is that having taken it up he delivered William Burton a blow of such venom that he was killed instantly. In court, Moverley was ably defended and his defence of provocation was accepted by the court. The judge, taking an extremely lenient view, sentenced him to one month in prison.

1907   Like a gunslinger of old, Harold Carr (aged 21) strode out into the centre of Mexborough High Street, calmly drew a gun from his belt and pointed it at three policemen whom he knew very well. He singled out the officer at the centre of the trio, Sergeant Matthews, and shouted, 'Now Matthews, I've come to meet you and kill you.' Then he fired one shot, which hit the policeman in the right breast knocking him to the ground. Warning the two flanking constables, PCs Haigh and Burrows, to stay where they were, Carr then turned and ran. But the two young officers were not about to let him escape and, blowing whistles to summon help, immediately gave chase.

27 NOVEMBER

Within minutes they were beginning to overhaul their unfit quarry and just as the faster of the two, PC Haigh, was about to stretch out a hand, Carr stopped and almost in one action, turned and fired. The bullet struck the third breast-button of Haigh's tunic, which saved his life, but knocked him off his feet. This left only PC Burrows to continue the chase and as they turned into a narrow street Carr, by now flagging, stopped and with a more deliberate aim shot the policeman in the right shoulder. Too tired to run on, he was then overpowered by other officers who converged upon him from different directions, managing to disarm him just as he was about to fire for a fourth time. At Carr's subsequent trial Mr Justice Phillimore pointed out to him that had any one of the three policemen died as a result of the shootings then he would have been executed. As it was the judge sentenced him to fifteen years' penal servitude. He was eventually released in 1915 and after joining the army was killed in France in 1917.

1917   An account was published of an inquest held at Goldthorpe into the horrific death of Harry Kilner, a miner employed by the Barnburgh pit. On the previous day he had been decapitated after becoming entangled in a haulage rope. According to a witness a number of full coal tubs had come off the pit road. After unsuccessful attempts to pull them back on to the road using a traction engine driven by 15-year-old Sam Fletcher, Kilner had become frustrated, and took the controls himself. After managing to haul back eight of the twenty-six stranded tubs he leapt off the engine platform to go and help the young lad set up ropes on the remaining eighteen. Unfortunately just as he let go of the controls one rope, held taut, snapped and wrapped itself around his neck, dragging him back with considerable force and eventually wrenching his head from his shoulders. A verdict of accidental death was returned.

28 NOVEMBER

29 NOVEMBER **1927** Samuel Case (aged 27) was sentenced to death for the murder of Mary Alice Mottram, in the front room of her Sheffield home. The two had been conducting a secret love affair for some time. As a close friend of the family he had been able to meet her on a regular basis when her husband was either out or at work without arousing suspicion. When she told him that she was pregnant and the child was his he took the scarf from around his neck and strangled her to death as she bent forward to poke coals in the fire. It was an open-and-shut case. He never denied his guilt and voluntarily surrendered himself to police. After the trial his defence team mounted a novel defence claiming that a convict in a Manchester prison, William Hartle, had told the prison governor that it was he, not Samuel Case, who had murdered Mary Mottram. According to his story the two men knew each other and had planned a break-in at the Mottram house but had been discovered shortly after entering the house by Mrs Mottram. He had strangled her with a towel in order to keep her quiet. But there were anomalies in his story that did not match the evidence and the appeal was dismissed. Samuel Case was executed on 7 January 1928.

30 NOVEMBER **1841** Robert Nall (aged 30) was sentenced to death for the callous murder of his wife Mary at their home in Sheffield. Separated for over nine months and on several other occasions throughout their married life, they had just decided upon reconciliation. Nall had taken his wife to the Hull Beer and Eating House in the Wicker for some lunch and the two had appeared to be on good terms. But Nall was a nasty piece of work and a very jealous man. Days earlier he had threatened to put her in her coffin and as they lay on the bed together that is exactly what he did. Without any apparent provocation he took a knife and stabbed her below the left breast. The knife passed through the liver and into the stomach; the wound was fatal. Mary died quickly and for a while he lay beside her body. Then, almost on impulse, Nall decided to give himself up. He got up, dressed and was about to leave the house when his sister arrived. She went for help while he returned to the bed. Throughout his trial he attempted to prove that his actions were those of a man insane, driven by jealousy and the fear that his wife had been unfaithful to him. The judge destroyed the argument and told the jury that they could not consider Nall insane just because he had committed an atrocious act. The jury obviously agreed: Nall was executed at York.

A Victorian image used to portray the condemned man's last moments. It would form part of a broadsheet sold to crowds at the scaffold.

DECEMBER

The stocks at Whiston village.
(Rotherham Archives and Local Studies)

1 DECEMBER   1862   Newspapers told of sensation in the Acorn Street murder. One of Sheffield's greatest trials was reported by the *Sheffield and Rotherham Independent*. Joseph Thompson stood in the dock and pleaded not guilty to the murder of Bridget O'Rourke. A member of the Fender Grinders' Union, he had been identified as the man who had thrown the bomb through the bedroom window of a house rented by George and Harriet Wastnidge. Intended for them it had been thrown into the wrong room and picked up by the young Irish woman. Almost mesmerised by the sparking detonator she had been found by Harriet Wastnidge standing in the centre of her room holding the bomb in the palm of her hand, not knowing what to do with it. As the two women had passed it between them it had exploded.

Bridget died as a result of horrific injuries; Harriet survived. It was her survival that had put Joseph Thompson in the dock. Prior to that fateful meeting in the now bombed-out bedroom she had heard a commotion in the street and pulled herself out of bed to see who was causing the noise. As she peered through her bedroom window she saw a man throw something into the bedroom on the floor below. The man caught his jacket on the house shutters as he tried to run away and was forced to extricate himself. While attempting to do this he glanced up and she saw his face. She later identified him in a police line-up. After his arrest this jacket with its torn pocket was discovered in a cupboard at his home. Coupled with his membership of the union and his job having been given to a non-union member, George Wastnidge, there seemed little doubt as to his guilt. But a stout and able defence discredited much of the evidence presented by the prosecution case and after considerable deliberation, to the shock of the whole courtroom, the jury returned a not-guilty verdict.

2 DECEMBER   1875   William Smedley (aged 54), a table-knife hafter from Sheffield, stood in the dock before Mr Justice Linley and pleaded not guilty to the murder of Elizabeth Firth. A widower since his wife had died a year earlier, he had employed Elizabeth, a widow, to clean and cook for him. Living in the same neighbourhood he knew her straitened circumstances all too well. With all her three children under the age of 12 to support, it had been difficult for her to earn money, and this made her vulnerable. Using this vulnerability to his best advantage he gradually increased her workload and her pay. In turn this made her ever more dependent on him and his generosity. Within a few months the two were sleeping together and by summer he had asked her to marry him.

But the relationship had not been all plain sailing: throughout their short, intimate relationship Elizabeth had come to realise that William's three older sons, all by this time young men, had developed a serious dislike for her. Seeing her as an unwanted replacement for their own mother they had tried hard to break the two apart and for that reason she refused the offer. But William had been smitten and strove hard to change her mind, which inevitably led to arguments with his own sons and a developing strain in the relationship. Unfortunately as autumn arrived he also lost his sight. Suffering for much of his life from poor vision and despite an operation designed to restore some of his sight he had always known that it had been likely to happen. Unable to work and forced to live on 3s 6d a week, life became intolerably difficult. After splitting with Elizabeth and no longer able to hold down a job he had been forced to go and live with his married daughter. For a while his life appeared to settle down and all seemed well, with even some visual improvement as a result of the operation. Furthermore he appeared to be in all-round better health both in mind and in spirit.

On 28 November William arranged to meet Elizabeth again at her house. Possibly because he was feeling better himself he had decided that he wanted a reconciliation, but had made it clear to friends that he knew it would be difficult to change the young woman's mind. The two went out for a drink and created an impression on all who saw them that all was well between them. How wrong can people be? While walking her back home and without any known provocation, he cut her throat. She died almost immediately. Smedley could offer little by way of defence and was found guilty of her murder. He was executed three weeks later and gained the notoriety of becoming the first person to be executed within the Armley prison compound.

1910   An inquest opened on this day at the Phoenix Hotel, Rotherham, on the body of Willie Meara (aged 16 months). In the dock accused of neglect were his parents Thomas Meara and his wife Lily. They both told the court that the child had been well nourished, well looked after and kept clean. The medical evidence however showed the child had only weighed 16lb at death when it ought to have been almost double that, and was seriously emaciated. Further examination had also shown that the little boy had been completely covered in flea bites; they formed a circle around his neck, ran in a line down his back, and covered his right breast and almost all of his scalp. The coroner advised the jury that he would have accepted manslaughter as a verdict, but the law would not allow it, because it had been brought to court as a case of neglect. Therefore, he reluctantly accepted a verdict of death from convulsions as a result of that neglect.

3 December

1855   Sarah Gamsell (aged 21) stood before magistrates at Doncaster charged with the theft of one shawl valued at 10s, one bracelet valued at 6d, one shirt valued at 1s, one collar valued at 6d, one chemise valued at 2s, one neckerchief valued at 2s and one handkerchief valued at 6d. The magistrates, who knew her well, sentenced her to four months' imprisonment.

4 December

1880   Greasbrough farmer Thomas Marshall was fined £1 8s 6d for assaulting his wife Sarah. After returning home from the pub with another woman, the court was told, he threw his own wife out into the street, telling her to find somewhere else to live. Not prepared to stand for such disgraceful treatment she immediately charged back into the house, grabbed hold of the woman with whom her husband meant to replace her and forcibly ejected her into the yard. Incensed by his wife's reaction Thomas took a garden fork and, holding it to her

5 December

Variations on a scold's bridle commonly used during the sixteenth and seventeenth centuries.

throat, forcibly marched her back on to the street. Then, under threat of murder, he forced her to walk ahead of him through Greasbrough village, at the sharp end of the fork. In defence he told the magistrates that his actions had not hurt her any great deal, despite the odd puncture wound.

6 December   **1903**   Samuel Wrightson was sentenced to six months' hard labour and twelve strokes of the 'cat' for committing what amounted to highway robbery, after stealing a watch from a man in the street at Sheffield.

7 December   **1856**   The bodies of Luke White (aged 62) and his wife Elizabeth (aged 58) were discovered viciously murdered in their own house at Bolton upon Dearne. The

couple had been battered to death. Despite a lengthy police investigation no one was ever arrested for the double killing.

1904   Arthur Jefferies (aged 44) was sentenced to death for the stabbing to death of Samuel Barker. Both men were known poachers around the Rotherham area and part of what was known locally as the Holmes gang. After a falling-out between Jefferies and the rest of the gang it had been collectively decided to bar him from all future activities. Essentially this put him at the fringe of what he saw as his community. He threatened revenge. Barker ostracised him and a friendship that had spanned a number of years virtually died overnight. Throughout the summer tension between him and every other member of that poaching fraternity began to build and by winter it was ready to explode.

8 December

In November after a night in a public house Arthur Jefferies lay in wait for his one-time good friend and stepping out from the shadows as he passed, picked a fight. The two men grappled in a narrow passageway that led into the yard behind Arthur Jefferies' house in the back-to-back terraces of the town's Holmes district. As they tumbled out of sight of others who had been drawn by the sudden commotion, Jefferies produced a knife, plunging it deep into Barker's side and killing him. No witness actually saw the fatal blow but there were enough witnesses to point the finger at Jefferies and there was no doubting the 8½in wound in the man's body. Local police searched the Jefferies house from top to bottom but the knife was never found. Nevertheless it did not prevent him being charged with the murder. The jury at the trial returned a guilty verdict with a recommendation for mercy. It carried little weight and he was executed three weeks later.

Far left: Arthur Jefferies. *(Rotherham Advertiser)*

Left: Samuel Barker. *(Rotherham Advertiser)*

1841   A report appeared in the press of the funeral of Sir Francis Chantrey at Norton, his place of birth. In his last will and testament he bequeathed £50 a year for the education of ten poor boys of Norton, £10 a year for the education of five poor men and five poor women of the same parish. He also left £50 a year which was to be given to the vicar in order that his tomb be kept in good repair.

9 December

10 December **1859** Abraham Binney was convicted of the murder of his wife Hannah after a violent argument at home. He had beaten her to death with some sort of blunt instrument, possibly a hammer, because, as he said later, he could not shut her up. He was sentenced to seven years in prison after the charge was overturned to one of manslaughter.

11 December **1906** James Dagnall of Conisbrough was sentenced to death on this day for the brutal murder of bookmaker James Dalton and the attempted murder of Annie Dalton. After finding them both in a bedroom he attacked them with a cut-throat razor. He managed to slash the bookmaker's throat but Annie fought him off and escaped. The sentence was later commuted to life imprisonment.

12 December **1866** This black day brought disaster to Barnsley. Described at the inquest as one of the worst accidents ever to befall a British mine, it happened at the Old Oaks Colliery during the day shift. A series of explosions rocked the coal face, killing 334 of the 340 miners underground at the time. A rescue group, numbering 198 miners who had travelled in from surrounding districts, was caught in a second wave of explosions that killed 27 of their number. Barnsley was totally devastated by the news. A relief fund was immediately set up to help the 690 dependants of those killed – mainly wives, children and aged parents – Queen Victoria herself donating £200 and the Earl Fitzwilliam of Wentworth Woodhouse adding a further £500. In total the fund realised the huge sum of £48,747.

13 December **1863** George Victor Townley was found guilty on this day of the murder of a young woman named only as Miss Goodwin. Throughout his trial his defence had always argued that he had been insane at the time of the killing. The judge disagreed and sentenced him to death. This decision was challenged and later overturned and commuted to life imprisonment. In the public outrage that followed, the case was forced back for judicial review some six weeks later and the death sentence reimposed. However, in view of the trauma that Townley had already suffered this was again commuted to life imprisonment. It still did not save his life: he committed suicide two years later.

14 December **1832** On this day Sheffield went to the polls and over 30,000 people gathered outside the Tontine Hotel to await the announcement of the results. By 6 p.m., some 2 hours after polling had ended, the huge crowd became restless at the delay and some sections began to throw stones at the Tontine's windows. An hour later and with the crowd's numbers being swelled further, the Riot Act was read. Special constables began to push people towards the Haymarket and a messenger was sent to Rotherham to call out an infantry regiment stationed just outside the town. Three hours later a full-scale riot had erupted in Sheffield's streets with the majority of participants charging off towards the Tontine Hotel intent on storming the building.

The Tontine Hotel,
Sheffield. (Sheffield
Libraries, Archives and
Local Studies)

A detachment of the 18th Irish Foot, some twenty soldiers, was ordered to form line across the hotel's frontage and prevent the by now charging mob from gaining entry. The crowd was angered by this military deployment, and stones, bricks, bottles and anything that could be seized and thrown were sent hurtling towards the thin line of soldiers. Commanding officer Captain Graves, fearful for his and his men's safety, ordered the troops to open fire and to maintain a steady volley. Four men and two boys were killed and scores of others in the crowd badly wounded. Despite this, the riot continued throughout the city until the early hours of the following morning when detachments of cavalry from Barnsley and Kiverton arrived in support of the Rotherham infantry.

1889   Robert West was sentenced to death for the murder of his wife Emma while at Handsworth Feast. A travelling showman, he travelled the length and breadth of the country with his shooting gallery and Aunt Sally stall. Emma had never had a problem with any of that. Born to the fairground, she had grown up, like him, a traveller through and through. Already under pressure because of continuing money worries Robert West was finally forced to acknowledge that after nine years of marriage Emma had embarked upon an affair with a fellow showman, John Baines. West refused to accept Baines's denial and eventually Emma confessed. Throughout the summer of 1889 life for the couple became unbearable. West could not forgive the indiscretion; Emma desperately wanted to leave but had nowhere to go. At last, during the early hours of an August morning, West snapped. Taking a cut-throat razor from a drawer he reached across the bed and slit his wife's throat. He never denied his culpability, confessing within minutes to fellow travellers and finally to the arresting police officers. He was executed at 8 a.m. on New Year's Eve.

15 December

16 December **1842** Joseph Cook (aged 25) of Ecclesfield was stabbed to death during a drunken brawl in the middle of the village by the man he had been drinking with all night. Thomas Twigg was the local butcher and in a fit of temper, after a night in the village pub, he drew a knife from his pocket and murdered the young man. Magistrates at Sheffield committed Twigg to the Assizes on a revised charge of manslaughter, believing he had not intended to kill.

17 December **Old Yorkshire Beliefs, Omens and Sayings**
A flake of soot hanging on the fire grate is called a stranger. If on the top bar, it represents a man; if on the second bar, a woman. You must watch the soot flake and if it falls to the hearth, 'a stranger on the floor is a beggar at your door'; if it falls into the fire, 'a stranger in the fire is one whom you desire'.

18 December **1835** *Mail bombs found in Sheffield!* Three wooden boxes, all charged with gunpowder and primed to explode on opening, were delivered to the homes of three Sheffield businessmen. Despatched from Birmingham, they had arrived on the Chesterfield to Sheffield mail coach and were at first believed to have been Christmas presents. Fortunately for all three the explosive mechanisms had been discovered before the boxes could be opened. It no doubt saved their lives. Named only as Mr Miller, Mr Rose and Mr Hobson, the men were all successful cutlery dealers and ran premises on both Fargate and Snighill. Police believed either a rival business or a jealous associate had sent the devices. For the unfortunate Mr Rose a ten-day investigation eventually

Attercliffe Common, Sheffield, 1790. *(Sheffield Libraries, Archives and Local Studies)*

pointed an accusing finger in his direction, despite his own apparent brush with death. He, police concluded, had made the bombs to rid himself of business rivals. Undeterred by his protestations of innocence he was duly arrested and sent to York for trial. However, a jury of his peers disagreed with the conclusions of the police investigation and he was returned back to Sheffield three months later.

1840 Alfred Green liked watches, so much so that whenever he saw one he had to have it. When he appeared in the dock for yet another theft, the court was told how, after seeing John Richardson check the time by his pocket-watch while standing at the bar in a public house just off Sheffield's market place, Green had followed him as far as Fargate. Once out of public view he attacked the man, beat him to the ground and stole away his prize along with a few coppers in change. Unfortunately for him, however, the victim had seen his face quite clearly and a matter of only a few short hours later, accompanied by a constable, Richardson identified Alfred as he bought a drink in a local haunt which police knew he often used. The judge pronounced Green unfit to remain in this country and sentenced him to go and live in another one. He was transported for fifteen years.

19 DECEMBER

Conditions on board a transport ship. *(Hulton Getty)*

20 DECEMBER **1832** At Sheffield Town Hall Assizes Matthew Coe was found guilty of stealing four ducks and sentenced to be transported to the Australian penal colony for fourteen years. Found guilty alongside Coe and sentenced to join him were William Walker, for stealing a quantity of pigeons, and George Stephenson for picking a pocket of two gold sovereigns.

21 DECEMBER **1861** An atrocious attack on property sparked outrage at Thorpe Hesley. Two nail shops were blown up in Thorpe Hesley village by means of crude bombs manufactured using old tins and gunpowder. John Hattersley and Charles Butcher, the respective owners of these premises, were put out of business as a result and prevented from being able to carry on their trade as nail-makers. Suspicion, well founded, fell upon the Nail Makers' Union after it became known that the two men had ignored the union's threat that repercussions would follow if they did not join the union. The Belper-based union had a branch office in the village and several meetings had been held in an effort to prevent the men continuing to work for a rate of pay below that agreed by the branch. On the night of the explosion a young woman claimed to have seen the men who threw the bombs and identified Emmanuel Watson, James Watson and Joseph Tomlinson, all nail-makers from Belper and Chesterfield. The three men were arrested and accused of being the main conspirators. They all denied it and offered up evidence to show that they had not been in Thorpe Hesley on the night in question. But the evidence of the witness, despite the fact that it had been a dark night and no lamps lit, held firm. After a lengthy trial the three were found guilty and sentenced to fourteen years' imprisonment.

The nail shop at Thorpe Hesley. *(Brian Elliott Collection)*

1888 *The murder that never was.* Tramp Alfred Carter (aged 35), a one-time Sheffield baker, calmly walked into a police station at Richmond, North Yorkshire, and admitted to having stabbed to death a man by the name of William Hawkins. According to the story he told, the two had met on the road just north of Barnsley and after a drunken row outside the town the tramp had taken a large clasp knife from his pocket and murdered the man, eventually managing to roll his body off the road and into a ditch where he covered it with dead wood and decaying leaves. Barnsley police immediately began a search of the woodland area that matched the description and rough location of the alleged killing. Police at Richmond meanwhile arranged for the apparent killer to be returned south, where he was taken on a tour around the north-western edge of the town in the hope that he would remember the precise location of the murder. He did not and no body was ever found. Lack of evidence meant he had to be released but the question has always remained: did a murder take place that was never discovered?

22 December

1880 John Mills (aged 40) of Bolton upon Dearne was killed as he took his cart, pulled by three horses, across railway lines at Wath. Deaf since birth he was unable to hear the 3.35 p.m. Doncaster to Penistone train, despite having a young lad with him whose job it was to alert him to anything he would not hear. The young man survived unscathed but the train ploughed through them all at the Wath railway crossing.

23 December

1865 Reports emerged of an extremely violent garrotte robbery – highway robbery using strangulation as the means to fell the victim – in Broomhall Park, Sheffield. The victim, a Mr Burnby, had been attacked by two men and robbed of all he possessed as he walked through the park. He was severely injured during the attack and it was some time before police were able to obtain a description of those involved. Dennis Carr, Henry Smith and Edward Hall were all eventually arrested and charged. Hall caused the greatest difficulty to police and violently

24 December

Sheffield City Police, Eccleshall C Division, 1927. (*Sheffield Libraries, Archives and Local Studies*)

resisted capture, so much so that public subscription raised £125, which was handed to the successful detectives in recognition of their bravery and conduct. At the conclusion of their trial Carr was sentenced to penal servitude for life, Hall for twenty years and Smith, who the court clearly believed had played a lesser part, to five years.

25 December

Old Yorkshire Beliefs, Omens and Sayings
A crow flying about the house and cawing signifies a death to come, while to see one of the birds perched above is an omen of bad luck. A flock of crows flying from a wood is a sign of hard times and a crow seeking water at nightfall a sign of a coming storm.

26 December

1863 Attercliffe midwife Elizabeth Charleson was arrested on a coroner's warrant issued five days earlier for malpractice. Called out by her neighbour Ellen Athorne during the final stages of her labour, she had carried out a disastrous birth resulting in the death of the mother. The examining surgeon blamed her directly for the poor woman's death and she was ordered by the court to stand trial at the Assizes.

27 December

1779 *A Christmas Ghost Story.* In the *Lyonnell Copley Chronicles* is related the story of the ghostly apparition of Conisbrough Castle, a place where, in the dead of winter, people dared each other to spend time seeking out the Conisbrough ghost.

> On the night before today,
> In castle built of Conisbro' stone,
> Myne eyes have seen the phantom
> Of Abbott Monk alowne,
> In the castle with the candle lit,
> He was only in castel chapel
> Wore he dyd not syt.
> Ome at Mecesboro
> Bettey my wife I towld of the phantom and she spoke,
> No mower must you spake now of them fantommy folk,
> I was cauld,
> Caulder than fust men that deed and scayed,
> O pray for the cursed Conisbro' Abbott Monk
> That wrought this hour to me,
> May the lord take pity on hym
> And take me when I dee.

28 December

1928 John William Eastwood mounted the scaffold and was executed by John Ellis at 8 a.m. on this day. Landlord of the Bay Horse Hotel, Sheffield, he had taken exception to what he considered were inappropriate advances by barman John Clarke towards his wife. It caused a long-running quarrel between man and wife that went on for over two months finally culminating in Eastwood moving to Blackpool for a fortnight. On his return he took lodgings and the situation appeared to settle down. But it was a short-lived respite. On the morning of 29 July he walked into his landlord's bedroom carrying an axe, threw his keys on the dressing table and told him he no longer needed his room. Leaving the house he then walked to John Clarke's home on Lister Street, got Clarke out of his bed and struck him over the head with the axe as he opened his front door. The man died 24 hours later.

1903   National newspapers reported the Great Wombwell Mystery. Emily Swann (aged 42), mother of eleven children, had endured a troubled marriage. Husband William, a glassblower by profession, had a tendency to be violent after a visit to the pub and poor Emily was often on the receiving end of his anger and frustration. Over the years they had taken in lodgers to help pay the rent on their Wombwell home and the last of these, 30-year-old John Gallagher, Emily saw as a potential protector. She was attracted to him almost from the moment she first set eyes upon him, and the two began a secret affair shortly after his arrival. But Emily's husband was nothing if not cautious and that very caution made him extremely suspicious of their new rent-paying lodger. Within weeks he had discovered the truth and after a huge argument Gallagher was told to pack his bags and leave. However, despite the discovery he did not move far away and remained a constant, if secretive, visitor to the Swann household.

29 December

In June of 1903, perhaps tired of all the subterfuge, Gallagher told Emily that he was considering a move to Bradford. Horrified, she set up a meeting at the home of a mutual friend. Unfortunately for her on the night before

this meeting her husband beat her about the face quite badly. Incensed by the damage he saw when the two met, Gallagher immediately stormed round to her house and confronted her husband in his own front room. The fight that followed left William Swann with broken ribs and a badly bruised face. When the two lovers met again later that same day Gallagher was still angry and agitated, threatening to return to Emily's home and inflict even more damage. Emily encouraged him, telling him she would go back with him and help. He needed little by way of encouragement and that afternoon the two of them battered William Swann to death. His body was found within minutes of the pair leaving the house and Emily, who denied any involvement, was arrested that same evening.

Broomhill Police Constable Charles Swallow. *(Sheffield Libraries, Archives and Local Studies)*

John Gallagher was not found for a further two months. It was a straight-forward case and the jury at their murder trial returned a verdict of guilty. They walked to the scaffold together on this day and stood side by side as executioner John Ellis placed a noose around each neck. 'Good morning, John,' said Emily, from beneath the white canvas cap that covered her face. 'Good morning, love,' replied Gallagher, then, 'Goodbye, God bless you,' from Emily. The lever was pulled and the two were launched into eternity.

30 DECEMBER   **1852**   On this day Mr Justice Talford wept openly as he placed the black cap upon his head and sentenced Sheffield labourer Alfred Waddington to death. He had carried his 21-month-old baby daughter into Heeley Woods and cut off her head with a shoemaker's knife.

31 DECEMBER   **1913**   George Frederick Law was executed on this New Year's Eve for the unprovoked and brutal murder of Annie Cotterill. A lodger at the Cotterills' house in Sheffield, he had been ordered to quit his lodgings after two and a half years. The reason was never fully explained but he became extremely angry and initially refused to go. This in turn led to serious friction between himself and the rest of the household culminating in his landlord, James Cotterill, feeling obliged to remove all razors from his home because of an implied threat that none of them would be safe in their beds the longer Law stayed. It was a sensible precaution and a very rational fear. But George had only one target in mind. Two days after giving Law his marching orders the family heard him leave the house in the early hours of the morning. Believing he had gone to his work, James Cotterill clambered out of bed at 6 a.m. and made breakfast for himself and his daughter. Annie, his wife, stayed in bed because she complained of feeling unwell. From across the street, George Law watched father and daughter leave the house at 8 a.m. He then let himself back into the house, walked upstairs and strangled Annie Cotterill to death.